The Good Grave Guide
to Hampstead Cemetery, Fortune

© 2000 Camden History Society   ISBN 0-904491-47-1

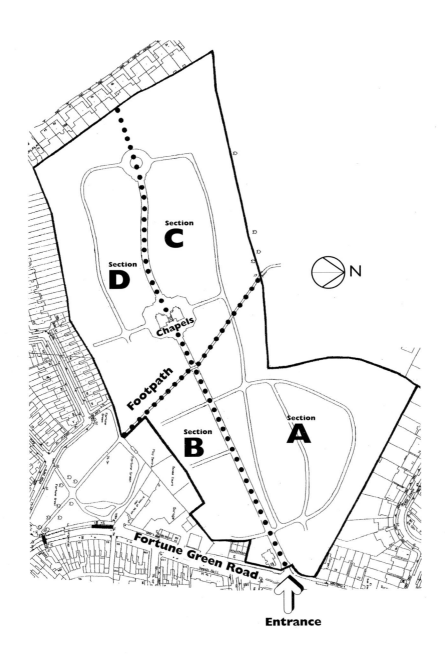

← *Opposite: aerial photograph showing location of the graves covered in Section A*
Graves marked with an asterisk have been Listed by English Heritage
Underlying photograph © by Aerofilms Ltd

Sources of information and of illustrations

Main sources

Barratt, Thomas. *The Annals of Hampstead*
    Adam and Charles Black 1912
    (reprinted Camden History Society 1972)
Dictionary of National Biography, OUP 1995
Series *The Streets of ...*, Camden History Society
    1972–1999
Who Was Who 1897–1996 OUP 1996
Camden Local Studies and Archives Centre,
    Holborn Library
Staff of Camden's Cemeteries Department.

Other documentary sources

J Fulleylove "Personal recollections of two
    Hampstead artists [Charles and Henry Townley
    Green]" *Hampstead Annual 1901*, pp 94–105
Edith Lyttleton *Florence Upton* Longmans Green, 1926
Justin McCarthy *Reminiscences* Chatto & Windus, 1899
F T Shore *Sir Charles Wyndham* Bodley Head, 1908
A Logan Turner *Joseph, Baron Lister* Oliver & Boyd,
    1927

Illustrations

We are most grateful to the following for
their courtesy in providing and/or giving permission
to publish illustrations in this publication.
    All illustrations are copyright.

Australian High Commission (Fisher)
Automobile Association (Sir Stenson Cooke,
    from sketches by Count Grixoni)
Bournemouth Borough Council (Long)
Camden Local Studies and Archives Centre
    (Greenaway)
Marianne Colloms (Cooper, Hengler
    programme, Irving & Baird, Terry & Neilson,
    Wyndham and Moore, Miss Storey)
EMI Archives (Barraud, Gaisberg)
Brent Elliott (Fischer)
J S Farley Monumental Masons (Bianchi)
A France & Son (Marie Lloyd's funeral)
Margery Gretton (Frankau memorial,
    Goscombe John, Pasha Wilson's tomb)
The Powell Cotton Museum (Cotton)
The Protestant Truth Society (Kensit)
George Ronald, Publisher (Blomfield)
Royal Academy of Arts (Dicksee)
Royal College of Music (Bache, Brain,
    MacFarren, Smart, Wynne)
Benjamin Stone (Cremer)

A note on 'missing persons'

Several people stated in other publications about Hampstead Cemetery to be buried here are in fact interred elsewhere, for instance **Fred Archer**, jockey, who committed suicide and was buried at Newmarket Cemetery alongside his wife; **Philip Dawson**, Secretary of the Railway Clearing House, who is buried in St John's Churchyard, Church Row, Hampstead. **John Braine**, author, is not buried at Hampstead Cemetery, nor is **Bernard Quaritch**, bookseller; the latter was interred at Highgate. **Blumlein**, pioneer of audio technology and **Thomas James Wise**, book collector and forger, were both cremated at Golders Green. The myths around the **Bianchi** memorial (Section A) are explored in the text. **Laszlo Biro** (also Section A) was not the inventor of the ballpoint pen but a talented film producer. Readers with a special interest in Poland should contact Dr Eugenia Maresch at the Polish Library, 238 King Street, W6, who has details of about 260 Poles who are buried in the Cemetery.

The Good Grave Guide to Hampstead Cemetery, Fortune Green

Marianne Colloms and Dick Weindling

Based on research by

Sheila Ayres

Patricia Barkley

John & Helen Brandon-Jones

Marianne Colloms

John Davies

Veronica Furner

Margery Gretton

Yvonne Melnick

Jean Smith

Caroline Sharp

Dilys Thomas

Andrew Tucker

Christopher Wade

Dick Weindling

Esther Whant

Tatiana Wolff

Line drawings

Margery Gretton

Editor

F Peter Woodford

Designer

Ivor Kamlish

Drawing by G A Storey RA of the daughter of the first superintendent of the Cemetery

Index to grave occupants

The initial **capital letter** (**A**, **B**, **C** or **D**) represents the major section of the cemetery where the grave is to be found. See the aerial views (maps) of the cemetery on the inside and outside covers. The **number** after the capital letter shows the position of the grave on those maps. The final, lower-case letter refers to the grid square in which the grave is located.

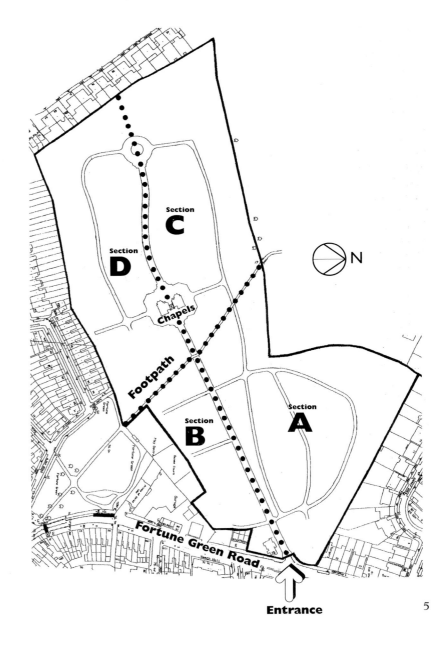

Section C

Section D

Section A

Section B

Chapels

Footpath

N

Fortune Green Road

Entrance

Introduction

When it became apparent in the early 1870s that the parish burial ground at St. John's, Hampstead would prove insufficient to meet the needs of a growing population, the local authority decided that a new cemetery was needed. The Hampstead Burial Board met in April 1873 and after considering several sites, settled on a 20-acre plot adjoining Fortune Green, which they bought for £7000 in February 1874. After the landscaping and the main buildings were completed, the Bishop of London formally consecrated the Cemetery in November 1876. The site was extended in 1901 by the purchase of a further 5 acres of land along its northern boundary.

The laying out and planting of the grounds cost £2500 and was carried out by Joseph Fyfe Meston, probably the most important landscape gardener working in London at the time. A number of greenhouses were built to provide plants for the Cemetery, but these were demolished in the 1970s and their site was used for the Fortune Green Playspace.

The Gothic-style chapels and the entry lodge were designed by Charles Bell (who is buried here). Made of Kentish rag and Bath stone, the twin chapels cost £4843; they are now Listed buildings. Key features include an open beam roof and stone corbels, while the design of the exterior stone finials was echoed in the original supports for the front gates and railings. The southern chapel was used for those to be buried in consecrated ground south of the main avenue; the other chapel was for burials in the unconsecrated ground to the north. The stained-glass windows, designed by local artist John Dudley Forsyth, were added in 1903. The railings along the front wall on Fortune Green Road were removed during World War Two, for use in shells and other armaments. They are due to be replaced as part of the Lottery Award to improve the whole site. The gates are modern and date from 1950.

Today there are over 60,000 people buried at Hampstead Cemetery and there is little space for new burials. The Cemetery is very attractive, with a wide variety of trees, including a large cedar and weeping willow, and there is plenty of wild life. There are many interesting graves and statues, such as those for Frankau, Wilson, Bianchi and Barritt, which English Heritage has recognised and included in a List of 18 monuments. These are shown as *EH Listed* in the text.

The Cemetery's own numbering on the gravestones is quite complex. Most graves (apart from those on the main paths) are numbered on a grid pattern. The rows run from north to south and begin with two single rows A1 and A2, followed by B1 in the NW corner of the Cemetery. The rows work across the Cemetery from west to east in groups of twelve, B1 to B12, then C1 to C12 etc. as far as the letter S. The recent burials in the paths along the southern boundary have been allocated the letter T. Individual graves are numbered down each row. On the more modern graves the number is often cut into the back of the stone, for example *G6/112*. A large section of the ground that was added in 1901 has been numbered as GLS. The graves on the main paths have a different sequence of numbers, which are usually found on the corner of their front edge. These main-path graves are designated WA, WB etc.

To help you locate particular graves we have divided the Cemetery into four sections. Section A covers the graves north of the main avenue as far as the public footpath which bisects the Cemetery. Section B contains the graves south of the main avenue as far as this same footpath. Section C begins beyond the footpath and lies north of the main avenue. Section D contains the graves beyond the footpath, south of the main avenue and Section C. We have marked the graves on three aerial photographs (see the inside front, inside back, and back covers) which show Section A, Section B, and Sections C plus D. Each of these has a grid overlay to help you to find the graves and the grid letter, a–f, is shown in both the index and the text. Graves marked with an asterisk have been Listed by English Heritage (noted as EH Listed in the entries).

If you enjoy this book, and your visit to the cemetery, consider joining The Friends of Hampstead Cemetery (contact the Secretary, 69 Fortune Green Road, London NW6 1DR).

Styles and symbolism

There are interesting monuments throughout the Cemetery, with a great variety of shape, texture and colour, reflecting the materials used. The most common memorial is the headstone, which can be found in marble, granite, Portland stone, slate, concrete and even ceramic tile. Some materials have weathered better than others. Perhaps the worst survivor is York stone, where over the years the action of water causes the surface to flake away. Some of the simplest and most dignified headstones are the War Commission graves near the two War Memorials, but they are also to be found scattered over the entire site. Crosses of various shapes and sizes are the next most popular monument. There are a large number of Celtic crosses, a style made popular by G C Maile (buried here), in his attempt to wean people away from imported stones and styles back to native materials and forms. There are a few examples of the Eastern or Orthodox cross, which is distinguished by three bars across the vertical.

Among the most impressive memorials are the box or chest tombs. They do not contain coffins, as is often thought, but are placed over a grave or vault. Many of the plots are edged with stone kerbs, or occasionally metal railings: metal chains were also used, but few have survived intact. There is one example of a wooden memorial, which consists of a length of wood fastened to two posts at the head and foot of a grave. Called dead-boards, bed-boards or sheep-boards, they rarely survive because the wood rots away.

Sometimes the desire to personalise a resting place produced highly individual memorials, prime examples being the sarcophagus-style chest tomb for 'Pasha' Wilson, who worked for the Egyptian government, and the Bianchi memorial, with its carved panels and poem dedicated to Matti Bianchi.

The Victorian 'way of death' was full of symbolism. Much of the ornamentation and even the shape of certain memorials carried meaning. Some are simple to interpret – for example, the use of a cross or an angel to mark a grave – but other memorials can reflect a complex combination of ideas.

The most commonly encountered carvings are the letters *IHS*. Various authorities interpret the letters as (a) simply 'Jesus' (first three Greek letters of the name), (b) 'Jesus, Saviour of men' (*Iesu Hominum Salvator*), (c) 'In this sign shall you conquer' (*In Hoc Signo [Vinces]*), or (d) 'In this [cross] is salvation' (*In Hoc Salus*).

Death appears in the shape of urns, and broken pillars. *Torches* reflect immortality or righteousness, and *trumpets* indicate resurrection and victory over death. *Obelisks* are well represented in the Cemetery and signify eternal life and regeneration. There are also a large number of *anchors* symbolising hope and steadfastness. *Angels* are plentiful, and figure in the most beautiful of the monuments. Some of these are shown as guardians, helping the deceased to Heaven. The carved flowers also have their meanings - roses signify beauty and perfection, lilies (purity and resurrection) and passion flowers (Christ's Passion and sacrifice) all frequently occur along the carved edges of headstones, sometimes intertwined with fronds of ivy, a modern symbol of friendship and immortality.

The Star of David over the Chapels attracts a lot of attention, but there is no record of any plan to set aside an area specifically for Jewish burials. It is possible that the sculptor intended to depict the 'Creator's Star', its six points representing the six days it took to create the world.

Epitaphs may reveal elements of the person's life – their rank or job, where they were born, lived and died. Some of the saddest recall the many children buried here; infant and child mortality was high in Victorian times. Lead letters were in common use until quite recently but they can be damaged by ivy, whose stems may lift the letters so that careless removal strips away letters along with the foliage. Other headstones have the words cut into the surface and filled in with paint. Older graves sometimes have a picture of the deceased carved in relief, e.g. the Maas memorial, while modern headstones may feature a photograph. The quotations are usually taken from the Bible or well-known poems and very few are original.

Some of the memorials were individually commissioned, but most are 'off the shelf' designs, chosen from a range on offer at a memorial masons. The nearest and longest lasting firm of masons was that of Robert and Richard Underwood, a father and son, whose business, opposite the gates, made way for a retirement home only recently. Underwoods is the name most commonly found on the front edge of a kerb stone. However, they may not have designed the memorial but ordered it from a wholesaler. As the Cemetery does not have a Monuments register, more often than not the identity of the designers responsible for the more interesting memorials is unknown.

In each of the four Sections, we have chosen to include people because they are known locally, nationally or even internationally. We also point out other graves because of their design or interesting features. We hope you will enjoy reading about the various people buried here and that this encourages you to visit the Cemetery. Use the numbered section maps to find individual graves that interest you.

Section A (see aerial photograph inside front cover)

This is our largest section and includes the graves of a number of actors, such as Fred Terry, Henry Brodribb Irving, Gladys Cooper, Clive Brook and Lilli Palmer. We even have the Queen of the Music Halls herself, Marie Lloyd. Russian royalty is represented by Grand Duke Michael. The range of people buried here is very wide indeed. There are artists, engineers, playwrights, religious fanatics, a ventriloquist, and a Prime Minister.

1d War memorial

During WW I it was decided to set aside a plot for free burial of armed forces personnel. The final memorial included a Great War Cross 14 feet high, erected by Dove Brothers of Islington in 1920. Around the walls of this well-kept memorial are the names of 112 servicemen who died in WW I. Behind the cross can be found twelve WW II graves; others are scattered throughout the Cemetery. (There is a separate memorial for *civilian* war dead in Section C.)

2a Edward Collingwood Andrews

(d. 7.10.1938)
WC307
Mayor of Hampstead
Andrews was a local doctor. He was educated at University College School, trained at Guy's Hospital and practised medicine for over 50 years in Hampstead. He was elected Mayor of Hampstead three times, and became a Freeman in 1935. He lived at 16 Heath Drive.

3a Jacob Arnhold

(d. 3.7.1903)
WB132
EH Listed.
The memorial takes the form of a well-sculpted and shrouded figure kneeling behind a pedestal, with one hand resting on an inscribed urn, the other supporting the head. Jacob's business address was East India Avenue EC, so presumably he was connected with import and export from that part of the world. He left an estate worth £82,994. Note the epitaph, *How good! How kind! And he is gone!*

4a John Alban Atkin

(d. 1946)
WD93
Chemist and Local Councillor
Atkin served as a Councillor and for some years was Chairman of the Cemetery Management Committee. He ran a chemist's shop, which his son took over, at 243 West End Lane. The only homeopathic chemist's in the neighbourhood, the shop finally closed in 1989 after nearly 60 years of trading. By then, the interior was like entering a time warp – with ceiling-high, glass-fronted display cabinets, large apothecary bottles filled with coloured water and apothecary jars with Latin names in peeling gold and red paint.

5e Nigel Balchin

(1908–1970)
WF29
Novelist
His *Times* obituary described him as an intriguing mix of skilful novelist and industrial psychologist. Born in Wiltshire, Balchin combined business, namely research in science and industry, with a successful career as a novelist. His earliest published work, under the pseudonym of Mark Spade, appeared in *Punch* and was a series of sketches on business efficiency, or lack of it, which he later combined as a book called *How to Run a Bassoon Factory*. During WW II he worked as a psychologist in the personnel department of the War Office and as Deputy Scientific Adviser to the Army Council, attaining the rank of Brigadier.

Balchin adapted his own work and others' for several 1940s films, such as *The Small Back Room* produced by Powell and Pressburger and *Mine Own Executioner*, which was a satirical attack on Civil Service bureaucracy, based on his own experiences. The only inscription on his book-shaped tombstone is from the title of his 1947 novel, *Lord I was afraid.* He died at his home, 48 Regent's Park Road NW1.

6a Francis James Barraud
(d. 29.8.1924)

N1/39

Artist. Painter of the HMV dog trademark

Francis became an artist like his father Henry. He studied at the Royal Academy Schools, the Beaux Arts in Antwerp, and also at Heatherley's. He painted genre and portraits and frequently exhibited at the Royal Academy. His best-known work is a picture of Nipper, his brother's dog, listening to the horn of an old gramophone. In 1899 Francis sold the picture to the Gramophone Company for £100, who reproduced it as an advert, and then adopted it as the famous trademark for HMV. Barraud is credited with giving the painting its title of *His Master's Voice*. He painted quite a few copies and when one came up for sale at Sotheby's in March 1998 it was expected to fetch more than £12,000. Numerous versions of the advert were produced for different countries, but in India, where the dog was thought unclean, Nipper was replaced by a snake! (See also Frederick Gaisberg, Section C)

7f Charles Herbert Barritt
(d. 21.7.1929)

WE291

EH Listed.

Organ-shaped stone (in the second row)

This splendid 7-ft high organ monument was made by Underwoods and originally included a seat (sadly, stolen in 1997). All the stops, pipes and sheet music have been realistically depicted, but despite this the sculptor was no musician – the notes do not represent a tune, they are just a jumble of pleasing shapes.

Nicknamed 'Clifton', Barritt died at 71 Ladbroke Grove. In 1910 he was working at the Savoy Hotel (his funeral service was conducted by the Minister of the Savoy Chapel). Later he became the publican of the *Blue Posts*, 6 Tottenham Court Road, a pub pulled down only in 1998. Although he was also an entertainer, we have not been able to establish whether or not he played the organ, so perhaps this monument was simply chosen for its visual appeal.

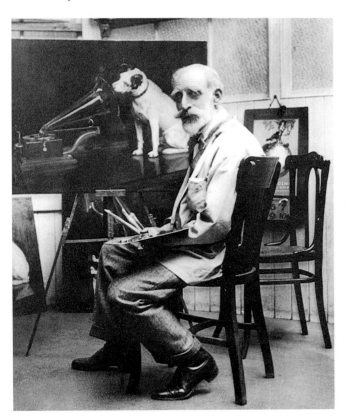

Francis James Barraud sitting at his easel painting the famous Dog & Gramophone trademark.

*The organ memorial erected over the grave of **Charles Herbert Barritt**, complete with stool (the latter has since been stolen, in an attempt to remove the entire monument).*

8d **Mattie Bianchi**

(d. 1936)

WH

EH Listed. Spectacular tomb with marble angel

Many myths surround this memorial, probably the most spectacular in the Cemetery. It is said to have been erected by a restaurateur in memory of his wife and baby. She was an opera singer who died in childbirth. Mattie, whose real name was Martha, came from Scotland, but we have not been able to establish whether or not she was a singer. Her husband was Cesare Bianchi, Chef de Cuisine at the Café Royal, and they lived at 21 Lawn Road. Mattie died shortly after giving birth in 1936, but her baby son survived her, and is not, as has commonly been supposed, buried in the grave with her. The couple already had a daughter, and some time after Mattie's death her sister Mary Gall came to London, probably to help look after the children.

The memorial was commissioned in Italy by Cesare and then shipped back to England in pieces. Farley's, a firm of masons based at Kensal Green Cemetery, assembled it on site. No cranes were used; instead, a long ramp was built and the angel was carefully raised into position. For maximum impact on the visitor the memorial was designed in the form of a triangle. There was once a small metal entry gate, long since lost or stolen, and the low walls on either side have also lost their railings. The two carved stone panels beneath the angel (artist unknown) depict the couple with their baby and Mattie ascending to heaven. Note the poem on the gravestone dedicated to her.

The Italian Government recognised Cesare's expertise and awarded him the title of *Cavaliere della Corona D'Italia* for work on behalf of the culinary profession. It seems likely he was interned as an enemy alien for a while during WW II, before being allowed to return to his old post at the Café Royal. Cesare and his sister-in-law Mary were killed in one of the last air raids of the war when a V2 rocket fell near Smithfield Meat Market in March 1945. Cesare may well have been buying supplies for the restaurant. 110 people died; contemporary reports say the market was crowded that morning because a consignment of rabbits or fish was on sale, a rare treat for Londoners used to strict rationing. Mary and Cesare were both buried on 19 March after a requiem mass at St Patrick's Catholic Church in Soho Square.

*The **Bianchi** family grave in its original condition, soon after completion in c.1938.*

9f Lajos Biro

(d. 1948)

WF150

Screenwriter

This is not the inventor of the ball-point pen, who was also called Lajos Biro. The Biro buried here was an eminent screenwriter and playwright. Born in Hungary, he worked as a writer and in 1918 was appointed as foreign minister by new premier Karolyi. In 1919 Lajos Biro, the novelist turned diplomat, was unable to negotiate a territorial settlement with the allies who invaded Hungary and Karolyi was replaced by a communist government. Biro accepted a position in the Communist Directory for the Fine Arts. However, this did not last long as the communist government collapsed on 1 August 1919. Biro fled to Vienna, where he continued to work as a writer with Alexander Korda. Biro went to Hollywood to conclude the sale of his play *The Czarina* to Ernst Lubitsch as the basis of the screenplay for the film *Forbidden Paradise*. In 1931 Korda moved to England to work as a film director and he asked Biro to join him the following year as a screenwriter. They made *The Private Life of Henry VIII*, starring Charles Laughton, which was a huge success. Between 1924 and his death in 1948, Biro produced numerous plays and screenplays which were made into famous films, including *Sanders of the River*, *The Scarlet Pimpernel*, *The Four Feathers*, *The Thief of Baghdad* and *An Ideal Husband*. Biro lived at 3 Telegraph Hill.

10f Sir Robert Blair

(1859–1935)

WE149

Education Officer

After working as a teacher and then school inspector, Sir Robert was London's first Education Officer, a post he held from 1904 to 1924. He was knighted in 1914 and lived at 33 Gresham Gardens, Hendon.

11c Lady Sara Louisa Blomfield

(d. 1939)

Q5/2

Author on Bahai thought and spirituality

Sara was the second wife of Sir Arthur William Blomfield ARA, the well-known architect (d.1899) who was vice-president of RIBA and architect to the Bank of England (1883). His works include many churches both in the UK and abroad; locally he designed St James' Church on West End Lane.

Lady Sarah Louisa Blomfield, writer and translator on Bahai thought and spirituality.

The Bahain faith was founded in Persia during the 19th century. Abdu'l-Baha, the son of the founder was, like his father Baha-ullah, a political prisoner in Persia for years. On his release in 1908, he travelled to Europe and North America to introduce his father's teachings. He summarised the Bahai faith in a set of principles that included among its social aims the abolition of racial and religious prejudice, equality of the sexes, an international auxiliary language, universal education, a universal faith founded on the assumption of the essential identity of the great religions, and a universal representative government. Abdu'l-Baha visited England in 1911 and again in 1913 and stayed with Lady Blomfield at her house in 97 Cadogan Gardens. Sara, who had become interested in a number of spiritual teachings, was introduced to the Bahain faith in 1907. She wrote articles about it and travelled around Europe to spread the word, and her position in society ensured that Bahain teachings reached a wide audience.

During WW I, Lady Blomfield and her daughters worked in hospitals in Paris and London. She served on committees and kept open house for convalescing soldiers from Australia and New Zealand. She also supported Mrs Pankhurst and the suffragette movement. When the war ended she made friends with Miss Eglantyne Jebb and was involved in establishing the Save the Children Fund in 1920. Until her death at the end of 1939 she devoted herself to Bahaism and published several books and articles on the subject. At the time of her death she was living near the Cemetery at 8 Burgess Hill.

12f Dennis Brain

(1921–1957)

WF166

French horn player with London Philharmonia

The grave is three rows in, behind that of Anthony Smith

Dennis was a child prodigy from a musical family: his father, grandfather and two uncles were all talented horn players. He was the soloist and principal French horn player with the Philharmonia Orchestra from 1946, and he gained a worldwide reputation. Several composers, including Benjamin Britten and Hindemith, wrote works for him, and his epitaph is taken from the latter's work: *My call transforms the hall to autumn-tinted groves, what is into what has been.* He would entertain friends by dashing off the *Flight of the bumble bee* with ease on the extraordinarily difficult French horn. At comic performances he even performed on the garden hose.

***Dennis Brain**, horn player.*

A great lover of sports cars, he was in the habit of driving to and from engagements in a single journey, no matter what the distance. Returning to London in the small hours from the Edinburgh Festival, at the height of his fame, he was killed in a crash on the Barnet bypass. He lived at 37 Frognal, the next house to Kate Greenaway's. Six graves to the right is his elder brother **Leonard Brain**, the noted oboe player.

13d Clive Brook

(1887–1974)

WF257

(In the second row, behind the large stone of George Duckworth Atkin)

Actor

The son of a gold-mining magnate and an opera singer, Clive Brook began work as an insurance clerk and a newspaper reporter. After serving in WW I as a major, he made his stage debut in 1918 and soon appeared in a large number of silent films. Brook had a good speaking voice, so he was still in demand after the 'talkies' were introduced. For 40 years Brook was a popular star in the West End theatre and cinema. He worked in Hollywood and starred as Sherlock Holmes (1929 and 1932) and in *Shanghai Express* (1932) with Dietrich. He returned to England and made *On Approval* (1944), which he also produced, adapted and directed. His last appearance was in the film *The List of Adrian Messenger* (1962). Although tending to be typecast in his early career as a reserved, sophisticated Englishman, Brook proved to be a truly versatile actor, his performances possessing "power, authority and polish".

Brook lived at Squire's Mount, Hampstead in the 1930s and towards the end of his life at 95 Eaton Square. He was married to the actress Mildred Evelyn and their children, Faith and Lyndon, both became actors. In 1936 Brook was the victim of a burglary when a quantity of silver was stolen. The man who bought a Georgian cup worth upwards of £100 from a shop on Kilburn High Road for just £4-15-0 later said in court "I thought it was a gift from God that is sent to antique dealers at times to cheer their lives"!

14c John Brown

(1830–1922)

WD118

Congregational Minister. Biographer of John Bunyan

Brown was minister of the Bunyan Church at Bedford for the greater part of his professional life (1864–1903) and among his publications was *John Bunyan, his Life, Times and Works* (1885). The economist John Maynard Keynes was his grandson. Brown lived at 10 Upper Park Road.

15c Rev. Alfred Cave
(d. 19.12.1900)
WC339
Principal of Hackney College, Hampstead
The *Dictionary of National Biography* calls him a *Congregational divine*. Born in London in 1847, Alfred was one of seven children. He was brought up by his widowed mother, a deeply religious woman who always intended her son to enter the Church. However, Alfred chose to study medicine on leaving the Philological School, Marylebone Road, but after a serious and nearly fatal illness, he decided after all to become a minister. Graduating from New College (Swiss Cottage) in 1872, he took up a pastorate in Berkhamsted where he met his future wife, and they later moved to a second post in Watford. However, ill health forced Alfred's resignation from both these positions.

He had become well known for his theological writings and in December 1880 was invited to become Professor of Hebrew and Church History at Hackney College. A year later he was appointed Principal. Problems caused by the growing numbers of students and inadequate accommodation at the College's premises indicated the need for quieter and more spacious surroundings. In 1887 the College moved to a site in Finchley Road on the corner of Parsifal Road. (Today the building is occupied by the Open University.)

Cave wrote a large number of theological books published between 1877 and 1894, and *The Story of the Founding of Hackney College* in 1898. In addition to his work at the College, Cave was also a director of the London Missionary Society. (See also **Garvie, A.37**)

16f Sir Charles Raitt Cleveland
(1866–1929)
WE142
Civil servant in India
Sir Charles was the Inspector General of Indian Police and Prisons in the Central Provinces from 1901 to 1910, when he became Director of Central Intelligence, India. He retired from India in 1919, returned to England and lived at 52 Pattison Road.

17a William Downie Cochrane
(1845–1892)
WC311
First Superintendent of Hampstead Cemetery
Born in Kirkcaldy, Cochrane was well qualified to carry out the work at Hampstead; he beat five other men to the post. Trained as a gardener and botanist, he had previously worked on the estates of Lady Keith, the Marquis of Lothian and Sir Coutts Lindsay. He was the Registrar and Superintendent at Bingley Cemetery, Leeds when he applied for the London job. This was advertised at a salary of £110 a year, "with residence, coals, and gas. The person ... must be between the ages of 25 and 40 years, must write a good hand, and be able to keep ordinary accounts, understanding Gardening, Excavating and Digging Graves". Under his watchful eye Hampstead Cemetery soon gained a reputation for good landscaping and attractive planting. A drawing of his daughter is reproduced on this book's title page. When he died in 1892 his eldest son, William Alexander Cochrane, who was already employed at the Cemetery, took over his post. However, he was dismissed in 1927 for embezzling Cemetery funds and is not buried in the family grave.

18c Mary Ann Cole
(d. 10.9.1887)
WB66
Founder and Director of Mount Hermon Orphan Homes
Miss Cole was the founder and director of the Mount Hermon Girls' Orphan Homes in Cambridge Road, Kilburn and at Praise Cottage, Mill Lane, West Hampstead. An advert in the Hampstead directory for 1885 says "Destitute orphans are admitted free, whenever a vacancy and funds permit. The work is Protestant and non-denominational. The children are brought up in the nurture and admonition of the Lord. 112 orphans are now maintained and educated. To any Guardian wishing to support an orphan in the Home, the cost is £14 per year." The 1891 census recorded 13 girls under the care of the matron and governess in the Mill Lane House.

19a Joseph Chicken College

(d. 1900)
N5/20

Unusual name

Nothing is known about the splendidly named J. Chicken College, except that he was a resident of Brisbane, Australia. In England, Chicken appears as a surname in the Northumberland and Durham area and it is possible that this was a family name.

20f Sir Stenson Cooke

(1874–1942)
WF279

Automobile Association's Secretary and Chief Executive

Cooke made the A.A. what it is today. Appointed as Secretary soon after the organisation was founded in 1905, he remained in post until his death. During that time the A.A. expanded from a single room at 18 Fleet Street with just 90 members, to occupy headquarters which eventually took up the whole of one side of Leicester Square (Fanum House, begun 1924, completed 1959). Coincidentally, Ernest Owers (see **A.58**) was also an early motoring enthusiast and a founder member of the competing motoring organisation, the RAC, where his membership number was 170.

Sir Stenson Cooke painted by Count Grixoni.

In 1905 *Automobilism*, as it was then called, was still in its infancy when Cooke was asked to think up ideas for evading the first police speed traps. He organised a number of 'scouts' on cycles who checked for traps and then saluted any A.A. member they met as a warning of what lay ahead! These scouts later evolved into the road patrols. Alternatively, A.A. garages would hoist a ball to the end of a pole where it could be easily seen and act as a warning to passing motorists.

Cooke was also a talented fencer and a member of the British Olympic Team in 1912, winning the British Amateur Championship in 1923. He lived in Muswell Hill before WW II, later moving to Stockleigh Hall, Regent's Park but at the time of his death was resident in Guildford where the A.A. was based during the war years. Strangely, his simple gravestone at Hampstead makes no mention of either his rank or his achievements.

21a Dame Gladys Cooper

(1888–1971)
WA171

Actress

Gladys was born in Lewisham, south London. Her father Charles Frederick Cooper was a journalist and founding editor of *The Epicure*, a food and drink magazine. Even though he also worked as a theatre critic, Charles was initially opposed to the idea of Gladys becoming an actress.

*Dame **Gladys Cooper**, the favourite pin-up of the British Army during WW I.*

Her first husband was Herbert John Buckmaster (Buck), whom she married in 1908 and divorced in 1921. She next married Sir Neville Pearson, some 10 years her junior, in 1928. Gladys had often done charity work for St Dunstan's, the hospital for the blind started and managed for many years by his father, Sir Arthur Pearson (see **A.61**). The couple set up home at 1–2 The Grove, Highgate, but the marriage was not a success. In 1934 while on a tour of the US, Gladys met an English actor, Philip Merivale. The couple married in 1937 –hence the name on her tombstone. In order to keep custody of her daughter, Gladys had been forced to allow Pearson to divorce her and not the other way round, which was considered the 'gentlemanly' thing to do at the time. Philip was the love of Gladys's life, but sadly he died at Los Angeles in March 1946 of heart failure.

Gladys was a popular actress on both stage and screen. She began her career as a photographic model at the age of 7 and was still acting at 81. In 1906 she was in the chorus line of the Gaiety Girls and went on to become an actress-manager of the Playhouse Theatre. During WW I she was the favourite pin-up of the British Army. She later gained fame in *The Second Mrs Tanqueray* (1922) and appeared with Olivier in *The Rats of Norway* (1933). Between 1940 and 1967 she worked in 30 films, including *My Fair Lady* and again with Olivier in Hitchcock's *Rebecca*. Her son was the actor Robert Morley and her grandson is Sheridan Morley, theatre critic, journalist and author.

When Gladys Cooper's father died the family wanted him buried in Hampstead Cemetery, although they did not live locally. Her mother and two sisters are also buried here. Gladys died at her home in Henley-on-Thames after a bout of pneumonia. The epitaph on the gravestone is a quotation from Spenser's *The Fairie Queene*: "Sleepe after toyle, port after stormie seas, ease after warre, death after life, dost greatly please".

22d John Crompton
(1854–1927)
WE103/4
Master of Heatherley's Art School
Heatherley's was founded by a group of students in 1854 and is the oldest independent art school in London. After moving to a number of different sites it is now in Chelsea. Former students include Burne-Jones, Rossetti, Millais, Frederick Leighton and Sickert.

23a Alfred Davies
(d. 27.9.1907)
WC316
MP for Carmarthen
Alfred was born in London in 1848, the son of Rev. John Davies, a Welsh Congregational Minister. Alfred became a member of the first LCC, serving from 1889 to 1892. Then he was elected as MP for Carmarthen for 1900–1906. He was the founder and chairman of the international carriers Davies, Turner and Co, with offices in London, Liverpool, New York, Boston and Philadelphia. He lived at The Lothians, 2 Fitzjohn's Avenue, and at The Copners, Homer Green, Bucks.

Alfred Woodham Davies (d. 21.2.1907)
Also in this grave is Alfred Woodham Davies (the son of Alfred) who was drowned in the wreck of the *SS Berlin*, off the Hook of Holland in 1907, just 7 months before his father's death. The *Berlin* was a Great Eastern Mail Steamer and left Harwich with its complement of 91 passengers and 50 crew on the night of 20 February 1907. The crossing was made in the face of a strong gale, but the *Berlin* had reached the harbour and was making ready to tie up when a freak gust of wind blew her off course, lifting the vessel up and dropping her across a breakwater where she broke in two. The fore part sank, while the aft part, with a few survivors, remained above water. All save 15 people were drowned, including Mr Davies, who had been staying with his aunt and uncle in Bishop's Stortford before setting off on his journey. A few days later, his body was brought back on the *Amsterdam* for burial in England.

24e Ardath de Sales Stean
(d. 1928)
WD150
EH Listed.
Died on SS Homeric
Here is another person who died at sea. The monument consists of a stone figure of a woman in flowing robes, balancing on a globe and reaching up to touch a flower-filled urn on a column. Symbolically the pose indicates a rejection of worldly pleasures.

25d Frank Debenham
(d. 1917)
WE241
(A large flat stone immediately behind that of Chief Smith)
Chairman of Debenham and Freebody (later Debenham's) department store
In 1778 a small draper's shop opened at 44 Wigmore Street opposite what was then still open pasture land. William Debenham, the son of a Suffolk farmer, bought into the business in 1813 and Clement Freebody was made a partner in 1851, having married William's sister. After the deaths of William and Clement, the business passed into the hands of William Debenham Jr and his brother Frank. Frank began selling small quantities of cloth at reduced prices to dressmakers who flocked to the shop in London to see the latest goods from Belgium, France and Italy. The business expanded and the new building on Wigmore Street was completed in 1907. Frank's son Ernest Ridley Debenham inherited the company, as William Jr had no children.

Frank Debenham's obituary says he was "one of the shrewdest and most successful men in the drapery business". He was a Hampstead JP, and lived at 1 Fitzjohn's Avenue, a house designed for him by J J Stevenson and now part of South Hampstead High School.

26a Eleanor Adgey Edgar

(d. 1926)
WC111
EH Listed

Nothing is known about this person. We have included the grave because it is an attractive one, with a cross and an inset niche which encloses a well-sculpted female figure in finely carved, flowing robes.

27f Maurice Elwin

(d. 1975)
WF233
Musician

Maurice Elwin, who started his career by singing ballads in his home town of Glasgow, became one of the most recorded artists in the world during the 1930s and 40s. His repertoire ranged from Gaelic songs to musical comedy and popular hits, which he recorded for different companies under no less than 30 pseudonyms. He returned to composing in later life, producing songs and film music. He died at his home in Canfield Gardens, aged 79. The main name on his headstone is Norman McPhail Blair; 'Maurice Elwin' is in brackets.

28c Cyril Arthur Farey

(d. 7.12.1954)
WC130
Architect

Farey was a Fellow of the RIBA. In 1924, with a colleague, he won an open competition for the design of Raffles College in Singapore. Farey and Arthur Edwards published *Architectural Drawing, Perspective and Rendering* in 1931.

29f William Bates Ferguson

(1853–1937)
WE138
Photographic chemist

Born and educated in Manchester and then Oxford, Ferguson was a barrister and QC. He was also a photographic chemist and invented a process of copper toning, as well as publishing a number of papers. He lived at 48 Compayne Gardens.

30c Walter Field

(d. 23.12.1901)
O12/14
Artist

Walter was the youngest son of Edwin Wilkins Field (1804–1871) a law reformer and amateur artist. His father's interesting maxim was 'Have one horse, and one hobby'. In his case the hobby was art, which he taught to working men in the 'conversation society' founded at his residence, Squire's Mount, Hampstead. His sons Basil and Allen followed the legal profession while Walter devoted himself to art.

Walter, a lineal descendant of Oliver Cromwell, was born at Windmill Hill, Hampstead. After attending University College School, he was taught painting by John Rogers Herbert RA, who lived locally in Church Row and later in West End Lane. Walter painted outdoor figure subjects and landscapes, especially views of Thames scenery; he also produced a few portraits. At first he worked chiefly in oils, but subsequently executed many drawings in water-colour. His landscapes and coast scenes show skilful technique. Field, a keen lover of nature, was untiring in his efforts for the preservation of the natural beauties of Hampstead Heath, and was the chief founder of the Hampstead Heath Protection Society. A drinking fountain was erected by his daughter on the Heath Extension in his memory.

Field produced a large number of works and exhibited a total of 42 paintings at the Royal Academy between 1856 and 1901. The Victoria and Albert Museum has two water-colour drawings by him, *Boy in a Cornfield* (1866) and *Girl carrying a Pitcher* (1866), and three of his Thames views are in the Schwabe Collection in the Kunsthalle at Hamburg. Among his most popular works were *The Milkmaid singing to Isaak Walton* and *Henley Regatta*, which contains portraits from sittings of many famous oarsmen. The 216 works remaining in his studio after his death were sold at Christie's on 17 and 18 November 1902. One is on display locally in the Burgh House music room.

In 1856 Field was living at his father's house in Squire's Mount. In the early 1870s he rented a studio on East Heath Road from the owner of 'The Pryors', a large house which was the original site of the block of flats now bearing the name. Field subsequently bought The Pryors, where he lived until his death in 1901.

31f Harry Robert Fischer
(1903–1977)
WF249
Art dealer

Born in Vienna, Fischer came to England in 1938 to escape the Nazis. He started the Marlborough Fine Arts Gallery in the 1940s and later the Fischer Fine Art Gallery in King Street, St James's, which he ran with his son. He played a significant role in advancing the careers of Henry Moore, Barbara Hepworth and Oscar Kokoschka. Fischer lived in Lower Terrace, NW3. His starkly modern memorial originally included a striking bronze tablet by Barlach, which has since been stolen. It showed three figures, one kneeling with upraised hands, one covering its eyes and the last seated, holding its head.

*The memorial to **Harry Robert Fischer** was originally adorned with this striking bronze plaque by Barlach (since stolen).*

32f Andrew Fisher
(1862–1928)
WE143
Prime Minister of Australia

"From pit boy to Prime Minister, from strike leader in Queensland to High Commissioner in London", was how he was described. Fisher was born in Ayrshire, the son of a coalminer and bee-keeper, and although it was illegal, he started work in the pits when he was only 10 years old. He worked in the mines for the next 11 years and tried to establish a miners' union, but prospects were poor. In 1885 Fisher emigrated to Australia, where he soon worked his way up to management level. He continued his trade union activities and was a founder member of the Commonwealth Labour Party (1901). He became deputy leader and then leader of the

Andrew Fisher, the first Labour Prime Minister of Australia.

Federal Parliamentary Labour party (1908) and served for three terms as Prime Minister of Australia. Fisher fully supported Britain in WW I, placing the Australian squadron at the disposal of the Admiralty and sending two divisions of Australian troops to Egypt and Gallipoli. He resigned in 1915 because of health problems and was appointed Australian High Commissioner in London, only briefly returning to Australia in 1921–22. He died at 57 South Hill Park following an attack of influenza.

33c Forte family
WD78–79
Hoteliers and restaurateurs

The Forte family came from Monforte, a hilltop village in Italy. Rocco Forte married Maria Luigia and in 1911 he emigrated to Scotland, opening a café in Alloa. His wife and son Charles followed 2 years later. Charles subsequently returned to school in Italy, but decided he wanted to follow his father's business. He studied book-keeping, started in a café in Weston-super-Mare and opened his first London premises, a 'Milk Bar' in Upper Regent Street in 1935. The successful business expanded to include the Café Royal and the Waldorf Hotel, and became Trusthouse Forte, a world-wide catering and hotel empire. Charles was knighted in 1970 and became Baron Forte of Ripley, in Surrey in 1982. The family lived in two adjoined houses in Greenaway Gardens. Both of Sir Charles' parents and other members of the family are buried here.

34e Frankau family
Arthur Frankau
(1849–1904)
WC380–381
EH Listed.
Literary family

Arthur Frankau was born in Whitechapel into a Jewish family. His son described him as "bad at games but a great gymnast, a tolerable shot, a good rider and a fine caricaturist". Arthur went into the family business started by his father, based at 30 Gracechurch Street. The company history is a strange one. Originally it imported leeches from France, but when they fell out of favour, it turned to sponges instead. Chemists were their main customers, and when doctors began advising patients to give up pipe-smoking in favour of cigars, the patients viewed the advice as if it was a prescription and asked their chemists for cigars, which the Frankaus in turn were happy to supply. Arthur died of TB in 1904 and was cremated at Woking. He left to his children, says the inscription, *the priceless inheritance of an honourable name.*

Julia Frankau (d. 1916), the wife of Arthur, was the daughter of an artist-photographer in Bruton Street. She was partly educated by Madame Paul Lafargue, who was the eldest daughter of Karl Marx. Julia and Gilbert had four children – Paul, always known as Jack, who died in WW I, Joan (actually christened Aline), the writer Gilbert, and Ronald, who gained fame as a radio comedian. Julia worked as an embroiderer and in the office of a Necropolis company where she addressed envelopes, but she went on to become a successful writer. She published her most controversial book in 1887 under her pen-name 'Frank Danby'. Entitled *Dr Phillips, A Maida Vale Idyll*, it was a vicious satire on Anglo-Jewish bourgeois society. *Punch* attacked it and said "It should never have been written. Having been written, it should never have been published. Having been published it should not be read". Despite the criticism it proved a great success and her best-seller *Pigs in Clover* followed in 1903. Julia also started and funded a West End Bridge Club, the 'Cleveland', and co-founded the Independent Theatre. A diabetic in the years before insulin had been invented, she died aged just 52, her condition complicated when she developed TB, like her husband before her.

Gilbert Frankau (1884–1952) After Eton, Gilbert joined the family cigar firm which survived several financial crises and diversified to include the sale of cigarettes. He served in the Royal Field Artillery at Ypres and the Somme and undertook propaganda duties in Italy, but was invalided out with shell-shock in February 1918. After the later sale of the cigar business, he pursued his ambition to become a writer and poet. Gilbert made his reputation with his second novel, *Peter Jackson, Cigar Merchant* (1920), clearly based on first-hand knowledge. Described as "a fluent, lavish author with a genuine gift for story telling", he was in great demand and his books were very popular, several of his novels being filmed. He disliked Socialism and socialist writers and in the 1920s he spoke for right-wing causes. In 1928 he became the editor of *Britannia*, a weekly magazine with Imperial sympathies. During WW II he served in the RAFVR and rose to the rank of Squadron Leader. He died on 4 December 1952 at his home in Hove, determined to finish his last novel, *Unborn Tomorrow*, considered as one of his best. Gilbert was married three times. There were two children from his first marriage, Ursula and Pamela, the author. Both are buried nearby.

Ronald Frankau (1894–1951), the youngest son of Arthur and Julia Frankau, is remembered but not buried here. Ronald was a radio comedian who broadcast in a double act with Tommy Handley as 'Mr Murgatroyd and Mr Winterbottom'. He was educated at Eton and studied at the Guildhall School of Music for a short time. He returned from Canada to join the Army in 1914. After the war he travelled in India with a repertory company and performed with concert parties in England from 1920.

The Frankau memorial has a fascinating history. Despite the fact that he was known to be unreliable, Julia commissioned Alfred Gilbert, the sculptor of Eros in Piccadilly Circus, to design her husband's memorial. (He

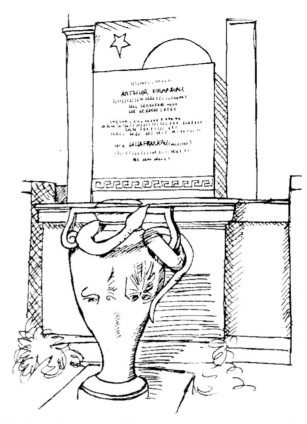

*The **Frankau** memorial complete with the bronze urn which was stolen in 1997.*

had a house and studio at 16 Maida Vale and lived there from 1893 to 1901 until bankruptcy forced him to move to Belgium.) Gilbert agreed to complete the monument in bronze, marble and granite within 6 months, the time limit imposed by Julia. She approved his sketch and agreed to a fee of 600 guineas, but for every day Gilbert delayed delivery, he was to forfeit a pound. It seems certain that Julia knew of Gilbert's reputation for not completing work on time, hence the penalty clause. The date for erecting the monument was set for the end of October 1905, and work began in May. Gilbert, then living in Bruges, repeatedly assured Julia that everything was fine. But October came and went and there was no memorial. Julia sent her solicitor to Bruges who was eventually allowed to see a rough clay model of the intended design, a sort of huge vase or jardinière with few details and standing some 7 or 8 feet high. "It is a sad sight" was the widow's only comment. Julia promptly asked Gilbert to return what she'd already paid, some £350 on account, but Gilbert had used the money to pay off his debts.

Unfortunately for him, Julia's sister was the gossip columnist for the magazine *Truth*, which specialised in scandalous stories other publications would not print. Julia threatened to expose Gilbert and despite his attempts at reconciliation, that's exactly what she did. The first article accused Gilbert of lying (amongst other things) about his ability to complete the commission on time. The affair was taken up by the general press and produced a flood of letters in Gilbert's defence. In particular the artist Charles Sims, who had seen the intended memorial formed in plaster, wrote describing it as "one of the most fantastic and beautiful that [Gilbert] has produced". Despite this, Sims concluded that Gilbert must have been dissatisfied with his work, broken it up and started again, probably producing the clay 'jardinière' the lawyer saw. *Truth* retaliated with a piece questioning whether Gilbert's artistic conscience should excuse him from completing work on time, like any other person who had signed a legally binding contract. George Bernard Shaw was drawn into the dispute and came down on the side of Mrs Frankau, although his letter was never published: "For Gilbert, if Mrs Frankau's story be true, shooting is too honourable a death. He should be drowned in the fountain with which he disfigured Piccadilly Circus. . . .I could at this moment get a considerable sum from any London manager by promising him a popular play to be ready by next October. Suppose I took it, and then said I really could not control my genius and harness it to the box office of fashionable theatres! Would you not say 'Then why did you take the money?'" It seems unlikely that Gilbert set out to defraud Julia Frankau. Probably he tried to complete the work, but lacking inspiration, gave up.

The artist who created the elaborate *art nouveau* monument finally erected in Arthur's memory is unknown. Sadly, in 1997 the bronze urn encircled by a snake which formed its centrepiece was stolen. A winged globe which originally stood on top of the urn had been taken previously. The surround and back panel are granite, with a silver and gold mosaic representing a quotation from Tennyson's *Crossing the Bar*: "Sunset and evening star, and one clear call for me". Gilbert described it in less than flattering terms as a "huge bizarre monument. . .more reminiscent of Constantinople than Tennyson".

35e Pamela Frankau

(1908–1967)

WA9

(Grave is two rows behind, across a grass path and to the right of Arthur Frankau)

Novelist, journalist

Regarded as one of the most popular writers in Britain and the US during her lifetime, Pamela is probably the best known of the Frankau family. She was the daughter of Gilbert and grand-daughter of Arthur, and both her grandmother and sister, Mary Wilson, were novelists. Pamela wrote over thirty books, mostly mystery thrillers, and her most acclaimed work was *The Willow Cabin* (1949). She is supposed to have encouraged herself to write 3000 words a day by repeating over and over again "Get on with it, you rat". Her memorial service was held at Farm Street Church, attended amongst others by Noel Coward and Dame Rebecca West. She lived at 55 Christchurch Hill.

36d Sir William Robert Fraser

(1891–1985)

WE126

Civil servant

Sir William was a career civil servant, in the Treasury, and Department of Health for Scotland. He was interested in tennis and held office in the Lawn Tennis Association. He lived at 33 Hollycroft Avenue, Hampstead.

37a Alfred Ernest Garvie

(1861–1945)

WD91

Theologian and religious writer

Born in Poland, the son of a linen manufacturer, Garvie achieved many academic honours. He became a Congregational Minister and wrote widely on theological matters. He was a professor at and later Principal of New College (1907) and Hackney College (1922). Garvie went on to act as Principal of the newly combined Colleges from 1924 to 1933, and was created Principal Emeritus in 1933. (See also **Cave, A.15**) Garvie lived at 34 Sevington Road, Hendon.

38a Charles Ginever

(d. 1946)

WC114

Unitarian Minister

Charles Ginever, a Unitarian minister in Stepney and Dover, was described as "a man of great tenderness and charm and at the same time a strong and unusual personality". Ilona, his wife (d. 27.6.1926) was born in Hungary, and was very fond of animals, as the hard-to-decipher epitaph demonstrates. Until recently there was also a stone dog nestling at the foot of the grave, but this has been stolen. They lived at 28 Belsize Park.

39f James Allison Glover

(1876–1963)

WE152

Medical Officer

After serving in South Africa and WW I he was awarded the OBE in 1919 and the CBE in 1941 for his medical work. Glover was a lecturer at the Royal College of Physicians and other Royal Colleges and later became a Senior Medical Officer at the Ministry of Health. He lived in Berkhamsted, Herts.

Section A

40c Cyril Gull
(1876–1923)

P7/12

(Grave is two behind that of Chynoweth on the path)

Journalist and novelist

Cyril Arthur Edward 'Ranger' Gull, to give him his full name, was educated at Oxford, and first became a journalist working at the *Daily Mail* and *Daily Express*. But he gave this up to pursue a career as a novelist. Under the name of Guy Thorne his novel *When It Was Dark* had a print run of over half a million.

41c Oscar Guttman
(d. 1910)

P6/2

(Seven graves in from the pink granite grave of Carlill on the path)

Explosives expert

A resident of Aberdare Gardens, Guttman was acting as one of several British jurors at the Brussels Exhibition, judging hunting and sporting equipment, when he was killed in a taxicab collision. Guttman was an authority on all matters relating to explosives, and from 1874 to 1885 he worked as technical adviser and plant contractor to several large companies in Austria. He later went into private practice in Vienna before moving to London and becoming a naturalised citizen in 1894. Guttman built gunpowder factories, gun-cotton and acetone works in many Continental cities as well as here in England. No religious ceremony was performed at his graveside; a simple service was held by a member of the Ethical Society.

42d Mordant Allen Gwynne
(d. 1910)

WE239

EH Listed.

Nothing is known about Gwynne, save that at the time of his death, he was living in 'King's Gardens' a block of flats on West End Lane. A pedestal supports two winged angels in flowing robes, helping the spirit of the deceased, as depicted by a central female figure, to rise heavenwards. The memorial bears the mason's name 'E H Mills of Hampstead' but it seems likely this firm simply erected but did not design the monument. For all its extravagance, it was probably an imported 'off the shelf' memorial from Italy.

43c Samuel Osbourne Habershon
(1825–1889)

WC329

Physician

Habershon was an eminent physician who began his studies at Guy's Hospital in 1842 and later became a lecturer there. He established a high reputation in abdominal diseases and became president of the Medical Society of London in 1873. In 1880, while senior physician at Guy's, he resigned his appointment, together with Dr John Cooper Forster, the senior surgeon. Their resignation was a mark of disapproval over the conduct of the governors and treasurer of the hospital in disregarding the opinions of the medical staff on questions relating to the nursing staff. Their action was recognised when over 400 Guy's men subscribed to a testimonial and presentation of silver plate to both men. Ironically, considering his field of expertise, Habershon's death was caused by a gastric ulcer. He was deeply religious and was a founder member of the Christian Medical Association.

Samuel Herbert Habershon
(d. 26.2.1915)

Also buried here is Samuel Herbert Habershon, the son of Dr S O Habershon. He followed in his father's footsteps, training at Bart's and later became Senior Physician at the Brompton Hospital. He published *Diseases of the Stomach* in 1909, clearly influenced by his father's textbook *On Diseases of the Stomach* which went through several editions.

44e Elizabeth Hagedorn
(d. 1945)

R6/11b

(No grave visible)

Elizabeth Hagedorn lived at 15 Ravenshaw Street from 1892. The story goes that her children considered her such a special person that when she died they erected a heart-shaped plaque to her memory on the house, which can still be seen today. The rest of the story is less clear. Her husband was supposed to have built some of the houses in the road but this is unlikely, as he was a tailor by trade. No.15 was also their second home in the street: in the 1891 census Elizabeth and Karl, both born in Germany, were sharing No.108 with two other families.

45f David Higham

(d. 30.3.1978)

WF265

Literary agent and novelist

Frank David Higham was born in London and educated at Harrow. Due to go to Oxford in 1914, he ended up in the army instead but was sent home after being wounded at the Battle of the Somme. Higham subsequently served in the administration of Turkey, resigning in 1924 and a year later joining the still relatively new profession of author's agent at the publishers Curtis Brown. Higham remained with the firm for 10 years before setting up his own company, which is still trading today. He gained the reputation as a tough negotiator on behalf of his authors and built his business into one of the leading agencies in the world. Among the many writers Higham represented were John Braine, Malcolm Muggeridge, Anthony Powell and Dylan Thomas. The firm also instituted the annual *David Higham Prize for Fiction* which was awarded to the best novel or book of short stories published in the UK that year. Higham returned to his old regiment at the outbreak of WW II and served until 1945. He was also a talented playwright and novelist; from the 1950s he concentrated on books of which *Expect Nothing* was probably his best. He lived at 12 Keats Grove and died aged 82.

46a Henry Brodribb Irving

(1870–1919)

E1

Actor

'Harry', as he was known, was the son of the great actor-manager Sir Henry Irving. Sir Henry had three children, all of whom followed him into the acting profession. In fact Harry went on the stage despite opposition from his father, who wanted him to continue his career as a barrister (he was called to the Bar in 1894). While a student at Oxford he did some amateur acting. Then overcoming the enormous shadow cast by his father, Harry first appeared on the professional stage in 1891, and made his name in the title role of *The Admirable Crichton* in 1902. Sir Henry saw the production and Harry nervously awaited his father's verdict. When the curtain came down Sir Henry praised a number of people and then finally said "Do you – er – *like* acting, me boy?" Despite his father's reservations, by all accounts Harry was a talented performer and he always said Crichton was his favourite role.

In 1903 Sir Henry appeared with Ellen Terry (his long-time co-star) for the last time in *The Merchant of Venice*. This was played by an all-star cast in aid of the Actors' Benefit Fund and it was the only occasion when Harry appeared on stage with his father. Harry went on to play *Hamlet* at the Adelphi in 1905, where his performance was described as a "brilliant triumph . . . worthily gained by thoughtful ability and genuine dramatic power". He went on to tour Australia in 1911 and South Africa in 1912. He also achieved success as a writer on criminology and published half a dozen books on the subject. He was also known as a good public speaker. During WW I he worked in the Secret Investigations Department of the Admiralty.

Also buried here is his wife **Dorothea Baird** (1875–1933), who appeared to great acclaim as 'Trilby' in Tree's production at the Haymarket Theatre in 1895. They were married in 1896 and had a son and daughter. The grave was described by a contemporary observer as "set in a rock garden overflowing with blossom". The verses on the stone were a favourite of Harry's by Arthur Clough.

*The actor **Henry Brodribb Irving** and his actress wife **Dorothea Baird**.*

Section A

47a Henry Arthur Jones
(1851–1929)
WC312

Playwright

Jones was a farmer's son from Buckinghamshire who became a popular playwright and a pioneer of realistic drama. Starting work at the age of 12 in a draper's shop, Jones went on to become a commercial traveller and wrote only in his spare time. Several one-act plays and a novel were rejected before the prophetically titled *It's Only Round the Corner* was performed at Exeter in 1878 and Jones felt confident enough to devote himself full-time to writing. His first major success came a year later with *A Clerical Error* staged by Wilson Barrett (see Section B), who also produced his celebrated melodrama *The Silver King* (co-written with Henry Herman) in 1882. This was followed by 30 years of unbroken success. His output was enormous – 60 plays, numerous essays and lectures, plus dedicated work to establish a National Theatre and, on behalf of authors, copyright for plays. Many of his plays were produced by Sir Charles Wyndham (see **A.84**). There was a family link in that his daughter Jill married Major Irving James Albery, Lady Wyndham's son from her first marriage. From 1910 to 1916 he lived at 6 Arkwright Road and thereafter at 19 Kidderpore Avenue.

48e Sir Bertram Lima
(1885–1919)
WF24

Newspaper publisher

Born in Rio de Janeiro, Lima was a newspaper man, and a workaholic, if contemporary reports are to be believed. His obituary noted that "he lived for his work. It might almost be said that it was his one interest in life". Joining the staff of Amalgamated Press as a teenager, he was soon spotted by Lord Rothermere and promoted to be his private secretary. Subsequently appointed Chairman of the Board, Cecil King described Lima as "one of the ablest servants of the Harmsworths", but specifically as "Harold's (Lord Rothermere's) man". In his twenties Lima was already in control of and successfully running the *Leeds Mercury* and *Glasgow Daily Record*, but it was as Chairman of the *Daily Mirror* and *Sunday Pictorial* that he made his reputation in newspaper circles. Knighted a year before his death in recognition of his war work for the Ministry of Information, Lima was also a member of the Canadian War Records Office, where he organised the photographic section. His obituary dwells on his professional achievements, but says little about Lima as a person, save to praise his even temper and courtesy. It noted that he was a very private individual. During the War he was a Captain in the Canadian Army. But Lima suffered a nervous breakdown in July 1919, the result of overwork during the war years, his health further compromised by a lung infection. Almost immediately after returning to work, Lima fell victim to the terrible Spanish Flu epidemic which killed millions of people at the end of WW I. He died of pneumonia two weeks after contracting influenza. His home was in Kensington but at his personal request, Lima was originally buried alongside Lord Rothermere's eldest son Vyvyan Harmsworth, "to whom he was devoted". Vyvyan had died of wounds sustained in battle just 12 months previously (see **B.21**). After a service in St Mary's Bryanston Square attended by Lord Rothermere, nineteen cars covered with upwards of 100 wreaths headed the funeral procession to Hampstead. Lloyd George, Winston Churchill and Lord Beaverbrook all sent floral tributes, as well as Lima's fiancée Miss Evelyn Lacon, to whom he had only recently got engaged. For some unknown reason, Lima's body was exhumed in 1925 and re-interred in this corner plot near the gates.

49e Marie Lloyd
(1870–1922)
WD14
(About 50 yards down on the left, two rows behind Brennan)
EH Listed.

Music Hall artist

Marie Lloyd was called the 'Queen of the Halls'. A cockney comedy singer, she was famous for her suggestive songs such as, *A little of what you fancy does you good, My Old Man said Follow the Van* and *She sits among the cabbages and peas.* When the police complained about the last title, she changed it to *She sits among the lettuces and leeks.*

Born as Matilda Alice Victoria Wood, her stage name was taken from *Lloyds Weekly.* Marie Lloyd first appeared on stage in 1885 and continued working until a few days before her death in 1922. She was born in Hoxton, London, the eldest of eleven children. At the age of 14 she was performing as Bella Delmare, at a music hall attached to a pub in City Road, London, for 14 shillings a week. Before she was 16 she was appearing in the West End and in 1886 she was earning £100 a week. Her fame as a Music Hall artist grew and even won praise from Ellen Terry and Sarah Bernhardt. She was incredibly popular throughout England, and tours of Australia, South Africa, and America showed that her cockney humour travelled well. She was married three times, to Percy Courtney and then Alex Hurley when the couple lived briefly in King Henry's Road. Her third husband was a jockey, Bernard Dillon. At the time of her death she lived at 'Oakdene', 37 Woodstock Avenue, Golders Green.

Overwork and domestic trouble hastened her end. Although ill, she continued to tour the Music Halls. At the Edmonton Empire, she complained of internal pains and a doctor was sent for. He suggested that she should go home, but she refused. Unwell on stage, she swayed to and fro while performing *I'm One of the Ruins that Cromwell Knocked About a Bit.* The audience loudly applauded what they took for very realistic acting, but as the curtain fell she collapsed in the wings and later died at her home.

On the morning of her funeral people came from all over London to watch her cortège pass by, many of them having walked long distances as they could not afford the bus or Tube fare. The police were on duty by 7 am and long before 10 am all the approach roads to the Cemetery were virtually impassable. There were so many flowers that over a dozen cars were needed for these alone. It was reported that 50,000 mourners lined the route from Golders Green to St Luke's Church in Kidderpore Avenue where the service was held. Over the next few days at least double that number filed past her grave, where a large space was roped off and people stood twelve deep. No burial at Hampstead before or since has ever attracted such large crowds and the police were called in to keep order. Legend has it that this was the last time the smaller secondary gates to the Cemetery were opened, presumably

to help keep the crowd moving. The epitaph on her grave was composed by her old headmistress. Despite her fame she left only £7,334 in her will.

The grave was purchased by Leah Belle Burge, better known by her stage name of Bella Lloyd (no relation). She appeared in pantomime aged 11 and became a close friend of Marie Lloyd and her family, appearing as 'The Sisters Lloyd' with Rosie Lloyd. In 1901 Bella married a boxer, Dick Burge, who was almost immediately arrested with several others for carrying out the biggest bank fraud ever known. He was convicted and sentenced to 10 years in prison, but Bella agreed to wait for him. She worked hard and by the time he was released she had enough money to buy the old Surrey Chapel in Blackfriars, which the couple converted. Called 'The Ring', its thrice-weekly boxing matches made a fortune for the Burges. After Dick's death in 1918, Bella continued to run it for another 21 years. In 1958, Bella was the subject of television's *This is Your Life*. She died aged 85 in 1962.

Marie Lloyd's funeral procession, shown turning out of Armitage Road and moving along a crowded Golders Green Road towards the Finchley Road.

50a George Charles Maile

(d. 1929)

WD87

Monumental artist

A student at the West London Art School, his obituary noted that Maile had tried to steer public taste away from imported white marble monuments by "adapting to modern use the beautiful early Christian Celtic, Scottish and Cornish crosses carved in stone from this country". The firm was based at 367 Euston Road and his own memorial consists of a simple tall tapering cross. Maile was also a keen supporter of elementary education. Elected manager under the old London School Board, he subsequently acted as chairman of the Hampstead group of LCC Schools until a few years before his death, aged 80. Maile lived in Corringham Road, Golders Green.

51a Charlotte Mary Mew

(1869–1928)

M11/28–29

(On the left of the path, first find Galea in the front row and then to the right Dunthorne, Mew is then five graves in)

Poet

Charlotte Mew was a well-known poet in her day. Among her admirers were Hugh Walpole, Robert Bridges the Poet Laureate, Virginia Woolf and Thomas Hardy, who described her as "far and away the best living woman poet, who will be read when others are forgotten". Her father was Frederick Mew, architect, co-designer of Hampstead Town Hall on Haverstock Hill. Charlotte, born at 10 Doughty Street, lived most of her life in Bloomsbury. She was one of seven children, three of whom died in infancy while two were later declared insane and confined to asylums. So she became very attached to her surviving sister Anne.

Charlotte had many problems – the family's fortunes declined under the strain of supporting the two children in private asylums. Both Charlotte and Anne decided never to marry for fear of passing on the mental problems which they believed to be hereditary. Charlotte's attraction to the novelist Mary Sinclair was rebuffed; it was alleged she told Charlotte that she was "wasting her perfectly good passion". Charlotte's life experiences are often mirrored in her poems – in particular, the asylum where her siblings were confined. When the lease on their Bloomsbury home was up, the remaining family members – mother, Anne and Charlotte – were forced to move to two rooms, two attics and a dark kitchen in Delancey Street.

Anne died of cancer in a nursing home in Priory Road NW6 in 1927. Her sister's death greatly upset Charlotte. She wrote "it was over at midnight on Saturday. And now she can never be old, or not properly taken care of, or alone".

When it no longer really mattered, Charlotte was suddenly a wealthy woman, through an unexpected family bequest. She became obsessed with the idea that Anne had been buried alive, and was admitted to a nursing home off Baker Street suffering from a nervous disorder. At lunchtime on 14 March 1928 she told the matron that she was going out for a few minutes. She bought a bottle of Lysol, a corrosive creosote solution, commonly used as a disinfectant, returned to her room with her package, poured half the bottle into a glass and drank it. Her last words were "Don't keep me, let me go". She had insisted that her main artery be severed before she was put in her coffin to make sure she was dead before burial. In her will she left instructions that a headstone be erected over her sister's grave with the inscription *Cast down the seed of weeping and attend*, which is from Dante's *Purgatorio*.

52a Grand Duke Michael Michailovitch

(1861–1929)

WC106–107

(Large tomb, behind Storey, in the second row)

Grandson of Tsar Nicholas I of Russia

This surprisingly plain grave is the resting place of His Imperial Highness the Grand Duke Michael Michailovitch of Russia, grandson of Tsar Nicholas I. Grand Duke Michael began his military service in the Caucasus, then transferred to Petrograd and served in the Russo-Turkish War of 1877. Princess Mary of Teck, who later became Queen Mary, wife of George V, was suggested as a suitable bride for Grand Duke Michael. But in 1891 he secretly married Sophy Von Merenberg, a lady with many royal relations who was also granddaughter of the poet, Pushkin. She became Countess Torby, but as she was not entirely of royal blood, their marriage was declared morganatic (restricting titles and succession). Their treatment was harsh, as the Grand Duke was stripped of his military rank and exiled from Russia. The decree of exile was later rescinded, but the Grand Duke chose not to return to Russia. Instead, after some years at Cannes, where they built up their fabulous Fabergé collection, the couple settled in England.

They first lived in Keele Hall, Staffordshire before leasing Kenwood House from the Earl of Mansfield from 1910 to 1917 at an annual rent of £2,200. They shared the mansion with their three children Nadejda (Nada), Anastasia (Zia) and Michael, plus numerous dogs. The house was upgraded to meet the grand ducal requirements: one large suite of rooms was completely redecorated, electric lights were installed along the drive and part of the stable block was converted into a garage. The couple entertained lavishly at the mansion, where a ball held in 1914 was attended by the King and Queen, who came again 2 years later to attend the wedding of Nada to Prince George of Battenberg (later Mountbatten), the Marquis of Milford Haven. A year later Kenwood hosted another glittering gathering, when Zia married Major Harold Wernher, who inherited particularly spectacular night's events.

The Grand Duke was a keen sportsman and, accompanied by his wife and daughters, opened the nearby high diving board at Highgate Ponds in the hope that it would be used to train Olympic divers. He created a cricket pitch and golf course in the grounds of Kenwood and had specially modified golf clubs made, with very long shafts and an extra thick grip to take account of his powerful physique. Today, however, the only visible remains of the Duke's stay are two small headstones for 'Bill' and 'Mac', two of his dogs buried in the grounds.

The Grand Duke asked the Tsar for help in transferring money from Russia, but with the Tsar's abdication Michael lost access to his own and the Romanov wealth, and the couple's fortunes flagged. Just a month after their daughter Zia's wedding they moved out of Kenwood to Cambridge Place, Regent's Park. Countess Sophie died in 1927, and her funeral service was held at the Russian Church in Buckingham Palace Road. It was reported that the coffin would remain there until a vault was ready at Hampstead Cemetery. A plot was purchased in January 1928 and the Countess was finally interred at the end of the month. Less than 2 years later the Grand Duke, who died at his home in York Terrace, was buried beside her. Their only son, Michael Torby, who was known as 'Boy', worked as a theatrical and fashion designer but showed signs of depression as he grew older. He died unmarried in Roehampton in 1959, and was buried beside his parents.

53f Sir Henry Miers
(1858–1942)
R9/35B
(Nine graves in from Stuart on main path)
Mineralogist

Born in Rio de Janeiro, the grandson of John Miers the engineer and botanist (1789–1879), Henry was educated at Eton and Oxford and went on to Strasbourg to study mineralogy and crystallography. He held academic, administrative and honorary posts in many leading colleges and institutions (Principal of London University 1908–1915, Vice-Chancellor of Manchester University, 1915–1926) and wrote numerous scientific papers. Miers lived at 18 Aberdare Gardens.

Grand Duke Michael *with his children Zia, Nada and Michael and family pet, on the steps of Keele Hall.*

Luton Hoo in Bedfordshire, where the Fabergé collection is currently housed.

The Grand Duke and his wife were well known for their philanthropy. In 1913 he donated a motor ambulance to Hampstead Hospital, and in 1914 he started a movement to supply the troops at the front with warm gloves. A year later he allowed Kenwood to be used as the barracks for the newly established Royal Naval Anti Aircraft Brigade, organised by the Admiralty. The staff were accommodated in the stable block. Sometimes the Commander would go across to the Mansion and over breakfast, which he described as 'exceptionally enjoyable', tell the royal couple of a

54c George Monro
(d. 30.5.1920)
WA80
Horticulturist

Monro was one of the original recipients of the Victoria Medal of Honour, instituted by the Royal Horticultural Society to commemorate Queen Victoria's Diamond Jubilee in 1897. It was given to 60 eminent horticulturists (later increased to 63, the number of years Victoria reigned). This is the Society's highest award and the number of recipients is strictly limited, as a new medal will only be struck following the death of an existing holder.

The son of a Middlesex market-gardener, George started in his father's business. In 1871 he founded a horticultural wholesalers which became the largest firm of its kind in Covent Garden. Based at Russell House in King Street, it sold fruit, flowers, vegetables and garden sundries. In 1901 Monro served on a Parliamentary Committee enquiring into the fruit-growing industry. Two years later he converted his firm into a private company under his sons' management and by 1907 the firm employed 155 staff in London, with branches in Manchester and Guernsey. It survived into the 1960s, following a move to Watford after WW II. Monro was also a generous supporter of numerous charities and started an annual concert to raise funds for hospitals. He lived at 96 Haverstock Hill, next door to Augustus Stroh (see **D.66**) and later at number 99, on the corner of England's Lane.

55f David Morgan
(d. 26.12.1937)
WF45
X-ray pioneer

One of the pioneers of radiology in the UK, Morgan's work so badly damaged his hands that he had to give it up. He joined the Cunard Line in 1897 as Examining Officer based at Liverpool, with responsibility for all the emigrants and other passengers to America. In 1910 he became medical superintendent and by introducing better equipment and more highly trained personnel, he greatly improved the standard of medical care at sea. He worked for Cunard until he retired in 1926 and came to live in London. Appropriately, the only wreath at his funeral was of blue and white flowers in the shape of the 'Blue Peter', the flag flown by a ship leaving port. Morgan lived in Hampstead Way, NW11.

Julia Neilson see under **Terry (A.77)**

56d Robert Nivison
(d. 1930)
WE217
First Baron Glendyne of Sanquhar

Born in Sanquhar, Dumfriesshire, Robert Nivison was created the first Baron Glendyne in 1914. A stockbroker and JP, Nivison moved to Branch Hill Lodge, Hampstead about 1901 and was probably responsible for the rather unattractive alterations to the exterior of the house carried out at that time. Members of the family lived at Branch Hill until 1965, when John, the second baron (also buried here) sold the 11-acre estate and house to Camden Council. The Lodge was converted into a home for the elderly and a housing estate was created in part of the grounds, the rest of which form a Nature conservancy.

57c Sir Tom O'Brien
(1900–1970)
WD125
Trade Union leader

Growing up in South Wales and starting as an errand boy, Tom became one of the great Union leaders. He lied about his age to get into the Army and served in the Dardanelles in WW I. After the war his union work began with the National Association of Theatrical and Kine Employees. O'Brien was twice president of the TUC and the Labour MP for Nottingham. He died at 57 Parliament Hill. His epitaph is from a poem by James Shirley: "Only the actions of the just/Smell sweet and blossom in their dust". On the grave the word *great* has been substituted for the original *just*.

58e Ernest Owers
(d. 1938)
WD174
Major estate agent

Owers trained as a solicitor's clerk, later working in the Stock Exchange before joining his father's firm of estate agents. In 1879 he started his own office adjoining the newly opened West Hampstead tube station. To begin with he would walk home each night to Shepherd's Bush, but he soon moved in over the office. Locals remember how Owers "used to dash about, driving a fast horse, a large cigar always in the corner of his mouth, with prospective purchasers of land". He bought one of the first cars ever seen in the neighbourhood. Owers was involved in many of the land deals and developments in both West Hampstead and Golders Green, where he set up a land-sales office before the Tube line opened, working from a hut. Owers lived at 288 Finchley Road, but after he retired in 1931 he moved to Brighton.

59d Lilli Palmer

(1914–1986)

WE114

Actress

Lilli is commemorated here with her family; she died in Los Angeles and is buried at Forest Lawn Cemetery. She was born in Poznan, then part of Prussia, but now in Poland, as Lillie Marie Peiser, the daughter of a surgeon and an actress. After training as an actress in Berlin, Lilli came to England in 1933 and had a few small parts before she appeared in Hitchcock's film *Secret Agent* (1936) with John Gielgud and Peter Lorre. She set up home with her mothers and sisters at 17 Parsifal Road, which they described, perhaps somewhat unfairly, as the "second ugliest house in London", allowing that there might be one even worse. Lilli appeared in films throughout the War. She was married to her co-star Rex Harrison from 1943 to 1957 and for much of the time they lived and worked in Hollywood and Broadway. Her second marriage to the Argentine actor and writer Carlos Thompson lasted over 20 years. In a long career Lilli appeared both on stage and in more than 70 films, including *The Rake's Progress* (1945), *Moll Flanders* (1965), *Murders in The Rue Morgue* (1971) and *The Boys from Brazil* (1978). She appeared with actors such as Fred Astaire, Gary Cooper, Clark Gable and Lawrence Olivier. Her last film was *The Holcroft Covenant* (1985) with Michael Caine. As well as being an actress, she also painted and wrote five novels plus a very candid autobiography which received high acclaim from critics, but not from Rex Harrison. The autobiography was called *Fat Lilly–Good Child* in the original German, but was changed for the English edition to *Change Lobsters and Dance*.

60a Rev. Joseph Parker

(1830–1902)

WB123–124

Minister of City Temple, Holborn

Joseph Parker was born in Hexham, the only son of a stonemason and deacon of the congregational church. Parker followed his father in the Church and became a talented preacher. He worked in Banbury, where he was ordained and organised the building of a larger chapel. In 1858 he moved to Manchester, where he was a powerful preaching force as well as a religious writer. After 11 years he was called to Poultry Chapel, London, which he accepted on condition that the congregation moved to a different site. His newly built chapel on Holborn Viaduct, called City Temple, was opened in 1874, and he remained there until his death in 1902. Joseph's preaching was praised for its strength and freshness, he had "a soul of fire". He was a popular and prolific writer, his main work being *The People's Bible*, which ran to 25 volumes. His urn-topped memorial was paid for by the congregation. City Temple was the only Nonconformist place of worship in the City until it was destroyed in a bombing raid in 1941, when a bust of Dr Parker was salvaged from the ruins.

61e Sir Cyril Arthur Pearson

(1866–1921)

WE178

Newspaper publisher and founder of St Dunstan's

Born at Wookey, near Wells, the son of a country clergyman, Pearson was raised in Essex, where his father was the vicar of Springfield. Pearson was an ambitious young man and he won a newspaper competition, scoring the highest marks by answering ten questions a week for 3 months. This meant cycling some 30 miles to and from Bedford as many as three times as week to consult reference books. His prize was a job as a clerk with *Tit-Bits*, a new type of popular paper, and incredibly a year later he had become the manager. However, denied any further advancement, he left to establish *Pearson's Weekly* (1890). By using ingenious competitions he won a huge circulation and started a number of other papers. In 1900 he bought out *The Daily Express* for a halfpenny and in 1904 he purchased *The Standard* and *Evening Standard*. By the age of 30 Pearson was the owner of a company with a capital of £400,000. But he was losing his sight and he finally went blind in 1914. An energetic and highly motivated man, Pearson refused to allow blindness to overwhelm him. He told his wife that he would never be *a* blind man: "I am going to be *the* blind man". In 1915 he set up a hostel for blinded service men on Bayswater Hill. This later moved to St Dunstan's, a villa in Regent's Park, which gave its name to the organisation. Pearson was President of the National Institute for the Blind; for his work he was created a Baronet in 1916.

Pearson died at his home, 15 Devonshire Street, on 9 December 1929, following an unfortunate accident. While taking his morning bath, he slipped and hit his head on the taps. Stunned, he fell face down in the water and drowned. A very large number of people attended his funeral described as "one of the most impressive seen in London for many years". At the Cemetery the chaplain of St Dunstan's held an open-air service accompanied by the band of the Grenadier Guards. There were so many wreaths that a large display was made of them on the front lawn. A wreath in the form of a Union Jack had the initials 'VOB' which stood for one of Pearson's favourite sayings, 'Victory Over Blindness'.

In addition to his work for the blind, he is remembered for the part he played in helping Baden-Powell to set up the Scout movement. His son Neville was married to Gladys Cooper (see **A.21**) and worked in the family publishing business for many years. At the time of his father's death, Sir Neville was living at 58 West Heath Drive. He and his third wife are buried here.

62c Arthur Prince

(d. 14.4.1948)

Q9/10B

(Nine gravestones in from Christopher Bray on front row. Faint inscription)

Ventriloquist

Arthur Prince significantly advanced the art of ventriloquism. In the trade he was known as *'the Master'* and was the first to perfect talking and drinking at the same time. Prince began performing at open-air venues in Wales, making his London debut in 1902. As he gained popularity, Arthur played all the main music halls and toured America and Australia. He appeared at the first Royal Command performance in 1912. His dummy Jim cost £3-15-0 and is buried with him, a fact recorded on the headstone. Audio recordings exist of their act, where Prince appeared in a naval officer's uniform and Jim as a 'cheeky bluejacket'. A few months before Prince died, he and Jim gave their last performance at the Finsbury Park Empire. Prince lived in Ravenscroft Avenue, NW11 and later at 23 Abbey Court, NW8.

Cartoon of Arthur Prince's 'Jim'

63c Robert Rae

(1823–1900)

WC326

Secretary of the National Temperance League

The *demon drink* was long recognised as the cause of many social problems, and temperance societies, which started in the USA in the 1820s, encouraged people to 'take the pledge' and never touch alcohol again. There were a large number of temperance groups such as The British and Foreign Temperance Society, which started in 1831, and The London Temperance League in 1851. Its formation coincided with the Great Exhibition, felt to be an ideal time to launch the movement since temperance workers from all over England would be visiting London. The National Temperance League was formed in 1856 from the amalgamation of two existing societies.

Rae was appointed in 1861 as Secretary of The National Temperance League on an annual salary of £200, which by 1867, in recognition of his success, was almost doubled. As Secretary he assigned routes and tasks to the agents and supervised them closely. The agents would be sent to the various societies affiliated to the League as well as to other temperance societies. In 1869 the League founded *The Medical Temperance Journal*, edited by Rae.

John Turner Rae (d. 14.1.1929)

John, who succeeded his father, Robert Rae, as the Secretary of the National Temperance League, is also buried here.

64e Henry George Randall

(d. 1924)

WD168

(In second row behind Ross)

Master butcher and property speculator

Henry and Thomas Gurney Randall (see **B.33**) were brothers. Henry was the youngest of the ten children born at Trenches Farm, Langley, Buckinghamshire. He came to live in Henry Street, St John's Wood as a young boy, and worked in a butcher's shop together with his older brothers Joseph and Thomas. Henry was later employed as the manager of Thomas's first shop in England's Lane, but he soon opened his own butcher's shop at 94 West End Lane, then No.2 Exeter Terrace. A second shop followed in Finchley Road, but this was demolished along with several other premises in the 1890s to make way for the building of the Great Central Railway line to Marylebone. After taking the Railway company to court, Randall was awarded the unusually generous sum of £7,000 in compensation for the loss of his business.

Henry was familiarly known as 'Uncle Nutty' or just plain 'Nutty' to his business associates. According to the son of a local tradesman, Randall always "wore a Mullercut-down tilted over his left eye, a brown tweed tail-coat of country style although no doubt it was made by an expensive West End tailor, and a button hole . . . [He] had the reputation of being a Man about Town". Henry was very successful in his chosen trade, but he also engaged in profitable property speculation. He worked with the local estate agent Ernest Owers (see **A.58**) and was the owner and developer of West Hampstead Town Hall in Broadhurst Gardens, just round the corner from his shop. This imposing building was municipal in name only; instead, it provided a convenient venue for a variety of local functions such as concerts, elections and local meetings and even served as a temporary home for St James's Church and the Hampstead Synagogue. It later housed the Decca recording studios and until recently provided storage space for the English National Opera.

Henry lived in the rooms over his shop in West End Lane. He died in 1924, aged 77, less than a year after his wife Annie had been buried at Hampstead Cemetery. The funeral service was held at St James' Church, where Randall was a member of the congregation. A fine brass lectern in the Church was his gift. His father is also commemorated in an inscription beneath one of the windows.

65f Ernest Raymond

(1888–1974)

WF223

Writer and dramatist

Raymond was ordained in 1914, but resigned his religious orders in 1923. He served in Gallipoli, Egypt and Russia during WW I. After the war Raymond became a successful novelist, publishing over 50 books. He was awarded the OBE in 1972. Two of his books with local connections were *The Kilburn Tale* (1947) and *Two Gentlemen of Rome: the story of Keats and Shelley* (1952). Raymond was a tall man and a familiar figure in Hampstead village, where he shopped almost every day. He lived at 22 The Pryors, East Heath Road.

66a William Robert Rider

(d. 1920)

WC308

EH Listed.

Rider was a local Councillor. This is an attractive grave, with an elaborate marble and bronze headstone with good lettering.

67e Charles Cowper Ross

(1929–1985)

WD21

Theatre producer, director and actor

Born in London, Ross presented many plays and revues, some of which he also wrote or directed, including *Harmony Close* (1957) and *The Gimmick* (1962). However, the best known was *Toad of Toad Hall* (1964 and successive years). He lived in Camden Square. *Who's Who in the Theatre* listed his recreations as squash, golf and starting businesses!

His epitaph is very amusing:
> *What will be said*
> *When I am dead*
> *Of what I used to do?*
> *They liked my smile?*
> *I failed with style?*
> *Or, more likely, Who?*

68c Reinhold Rost

(1822–1896)

WA58

Oriental scholar

Born in Germany, Rost came to England in 1847 to work as a German teacher. Four years later he was appointed Oriental lecturer at St Augustine's Missionary College, Canterbury, a post he held for nearly 50 years until his death. In 1863 Rost became secretary to the Royal Asiatic Society in London for 6 years. His work so impressed Sir Henry Rawlinson that he secured the post of librarian at the India Office. His power of assimilating languages has rarely been equalled: he had a working knowledge of over 20 Oriental languages. He published numerous articles and wrote several entries for the *Encyclopaedia Britannica*, including one on 'Thugs'. He died in Canterbury aged 74.

69d John Sampson

(1859–1925)

WE89

Company Director

Born in Cornwall, Sampson became Director of John Brown and Co. a shipbuilding company, as well as other engineering and electricity companies. He lived in Queen Anne's Mansions, St James's Park and in Folkestone.

Section A

70a Alfred Slocombe

(d. 24.07.1899)

WC310

Artist

Slocombe was a noted flower painter and etcher with the Royal Cambrian Academy. As chief designer for a firm of silk weavers he refined the art of watermarking paper to such a degree that his portraits of Prince Albert and other members of the Royal family were exhibited at the Great Exhibition in 1862. The Celtic cross and Welsh inscription are for his wife, meaning "Faithful to husband and beloved mother". The family lived in a house facing West End Green from 1874 before moving to Iverson Road in 1891.

71d Sir Allan McGregor Smith

(d. 1941)

WE120

Engineer, solicitor and MP for Croydon South,

1919–1924. During his lifetime, McGregor Smith followed an interesting combination of professions. Sir Allan's wife is also buried here. They lived at 9 Greenaway Gardens.

72d Victoria Modupe 'Chief' Smith

(1937–1984)

WE69 (Attractive bas-relief headstone)

The headstone has an attractive bas relief and a Yoruba inscription which translates as "Market woman of Ago Oko and Egba-Okeona, Chief of Ikija and successful business woman of Ido Ekiti". Victoria Smith lived on Shoot Up Hill.

73a George Adolpus Storey

(1834–1919)

WC300

EH Listed.

Artist RA

A portrait and historical genre painter and member of the St John's Wood Clique, Storey was not elected to the Royal Academy until he was 80. The Times claimed that this was largely because he never quite fulfilled his considerable early promise, when some critics saw him as a possible rival to the young Millais. His work included paintings and drawings of the local area. The model for one of his pencil portraits was Miss Cochrane, daughter of the Cemetery Superintendent (see title page).

Storey lived at 'Hougoumont', 39 Broadhurst Gardens. His daughter Gladys was well known for her war work, launching a 1915 appeal in the local press "for donations to keep up the supply of Bovril to those in the firing line". Note the attractive carved relief on the headstone of a girl rising upwards in swirling robes, her long hair flying out around her. This is from a pen-and-ink drawing by Storey called The Spirit.

74f Arnold Jacob Cohen Stuart

(d. 1921)

WE195

EH Listed.

C F A Voysey designed the memorial. The main octagonal pinnacled tower base has flying buttresses which support an inner central tower originally topped by a bronze eagle which has been stolen. Thieves sawed the bird off its perch, and all that now remains are its claws. The eagle was regarded as a symbol of ascension, because of its strong upward flight towards the sun.

75e James William Tate (d. 1922)
Clarice Mabel Tate (d. 1966)

WD153–155

Music-hall entertainers

It is surely no coincidence that the graves of Marie Lloyd and of the Tates are so close together. Clarice Mayne, as she was known professionally, was a well-known principal boy and music-hall singer. Clarice always referred to herself as 'This' and to her husband James as 'That'. He was a song-writer and accompanied Clarice on the piano. James' best-known work was the musical comedy Maid of the Mountains. He died a few months before Marie Lloyd. Clarice then married Albert Edward (Teddy) Cromwell Knox, one half of the comedy duo of Nervo and Knox, who appeared with Flanagan and Allen, and Naughton and Gold, as 'The Crazy Gang'. The Tates lived for a while in Sandwell Mansions, West End Lane and later in Gordon Mansions, WC1.

76c George Tawse

(d. 1893)

WB14

Local Vestryman and campaigner for Fortune Green

Tawse was a member of Hampstead's governing body, the Vestry – the equivalent of a local councillor today – and lived in Belsize Road. His epitaph reads "He initiated the movement which has resulted in the preservation of Fortune Green to the public forever". The movement referred to was The Fortune Green Preservation Society, which was set up in 1891 to prevent one of the last local open spaces being used as a building estate. This was a popular cause which attracted much support. Unfortunately, George did not live to see the conclusion, as the arguments dragged on until 1895, when the courts unexpectedly ruled that the Green was not common land after all and could therefore be legally sold. The residents promptly began fund-raising, and Fortune Green was purchased by the Vestry from the would-be developers 2 years later, thereby securing it as a permanent public open space.

77a Fred Terry and Dennis Terry
(1863–1933)
WA166
Actors
The younger brother of Ellen Terry and a fine Shakespearean actor, Fred was more famous for the light melodramas and romantic-historical plays he performed with his wife, Julia Neilson (see next). Fred began on the stage at the age of 15 and played in the companies of Herbert Beerbohm Tree and Sir Henry Irving. From 1905 to 1913 he and his wife used the New (later Albery) Theatre built by Sir Charles Wyndham for 6 months of every year. Many of their most successful productions were staged here, including *The Scarlet Pimpernel* (1905), in which Terry made his reputation as Sir Percy Blakeney. During a Zeppelin raid in 1915 he came to the front of the stage to reassure the audience and then continued the performance. He retired from the theatre in 1927. The couple lived for many years at 4 Primrose Hill Road; Fred died suddenly, soon after the death of his only son Dennis. Dennis, also an actor, was on tour in Bulawayo in 1932 when he contracted pneumonia and died. He was brought home and buried here. He lived at 12 Frognal Lane.

Fred Terry in his most famous role as Sir Percy Blakeney in The Scarlet Pimpernel.

Fred and Julia also had a daughter, Phyllis Neilson-Terry (1892–1977). She became a successful actress, with a career spanning more than 30 years. She appeared with her parents in several West End plays and established herself as 'Trilby' in Sir Herbert Tree's production in 1912.

Julia Neilson (1868–1957)
Actress
Julia was the daughter of Scottish jeweller Alexander Ritchie Neilson and Gertrude Davis. She studied at the Royal Academy of Music and met Fred Terry in 1889 when acting in a Beerbohm Tree production. They married in 1891 while appearing together in *The Dancing Girl* by Henry Arthur Jones (see **A.47**). Julia appeared as Lady Chiltern in the first production of Oscar Wilde's *An Ideal Husband* in 1895. Fred and Julia's acting tours together were extremely popular and produced large audiences through England and America. After Fred died, Julia stayed on at their Primrose Hill house throughout WW II, despite air raids and the noisy gun battery nearby. She retired from the stage in 1944 and died in 1957 after a bad fall. Her epitaph is "I have done my errand, now I go".

78c James Tomblin
(d. 1930)
O5/3
Major builder of houses in Hampstead
Tomblin specialised in larger and more expensive properties in such roads as Canfield Gardens, Maresfield Gardens and Heath Drive. He was elected a local councillor in 1915 but resigned in July 1916. A sad entry in the Council Minutes notes that "owing to the death of his only remaining son in France last week, he felt he would be unable to take any interest in public affairs for some time to come". At the time of his death Tomblin was living at 20 Heath Drive, a large house which he probably built.

79a George Careless Trewby
(d. 19.7.1910)
WC314
Gas engineer
Trewby erected the gasworks in Constantinople in the mid-1850s, working as consulting engineer to the Turkish government. On his return to England he became the engineer-in-chief of the Gas, Light and Coke Company and built the largest gasworks in the world at Beckton, East London. Unfortunately, the origin of George's unusual second name is not known; Alan Coren recently wrote "Would you get someone with the name of 'Careless' to build your gas works?" The now derelict Beckton buildings were used by director Stanley Kubrick in the 1980s to provide the Vietnamese backdrop for his film *Full Metal Jacket*. George is buried here with his wife and daughter (whose age is given as 101). The other names commemorate members of his family interred elsewhere. His eldest son, George (d.1953) was a Vice-Admiral awarded the DSO; Lawrie (d.1968) qualified as a gas engineer like his father, while the youngest son was a civil engineer killed in action in 1915. George Trewby lived at Fenton House, Hampstead Grove, from about 1884 until his death in 1910.

80e Richard Underwood

(d. 1913)

WB10a

Monumental mason

A short stretch of Fortune Green Road opposite the Cemetery was home to a number of monumental masons. The first to arrive and the last to leave was the firm of Underwoods. Soon after the Cemetery opened in 1876, the family moved into a pair of recently built semi-detached villas, Nos.124&126, on what was then still called Fortune Green Lane. Their yard was next door. In the 1970s the entire site was replaced by Westmount, a block of housing for the elderly.

Robert Underwood (see **C.19**) and Richard Underwood were father and son. Richard, who is buried here, was born in St Pancras, as were several of Robert's other children. As the firm was established in 1844, it seems likely that this is where it began. For many years the Underwoods lived and worked at Fortune Green but at the time of his death, Richard was living in Alexandra Road. He was a member of Hampstead Vestry for 10 years and was one of the founders of the National Association of Master Monumental Masons and Sculptors. Bearing in mind the family trade, it is surprising that his grave is marked by such a plain headstone, with minimal carved ornamentation. In a 1929 advert the firm offered a "free Art Catalogue of 100 designs in stock, ready for erection", so perhaps this was one of them!

Masons would often 'sign' their monuments, usually along the front kerb edge of a grave, but after 1926 this practice was abandoned, as many found this type of advertising not in good taste. One or two of the monuments do bear the very pointed inscription "Underwood, opposite the gates".

81d Dr James Howard Wellard

(1912–1987)

WE61

Writer and explorer

London-born, Wellard was educated in an orphanage and went on to study for his BA at night school. While working as a library assistant he won a Rockefeller Scholarship to Chicago University. During WW II he acted as special correspondent for the Chicago Times, travelling with the armies in Europe and North Africa. After the war was over, Wellard settled in Italy for some years, returning briefly to the USA as a visiting lecturer, before taking up a Fulbright Fellowship to the University of Tehran in 1958–9. In 1961 he brought his family to live in London and settled down to full-time writing and research. Wellard's books cover a wide range of subjects, both fiction and non-fiction. His trilogy on North Africa deals with the history and archaeology of the Sahara, but he also wrote detective, historical and romantic novels. Wellard made many TV and radio appearances and sold the film rights to several of his books; one entitled *Action of the Tiger* was made into a film starring Sean Connery. Wellard lived at 14 The Pryors, East Heath Road.

82c James 'Pasha' Wilson

(1831–1906)

WC359

EH Listed.

Civil Engineer

A mock-Egyptian temple in pink granite protected by a winged disc intended to ward off evil tops this grave, appropriate to 'Pasha Wilson', who was employed for 44 years as an engineer by the Egyptian Government. Born in Renfrewshire, Wilson was first apprenticed to Napier and Sons, Glasgow, later working for the Cunard Steamship Company. In 1857 he went to Egypt as chief engineer of the Nile Steam Towing company, moving to the service of Ismail Pasha a year later. He worked to improve agriculture and other industries, and was appointed Chief Engineer by the Egyptian Government (1875–1901), when he was primarily responsible for increasing sugar production. He received the title of 'Pasha' in 1895, the last of a long line of honours. In 1901 he retired and returned to England. Wilson lived at 19 Lymington Road and his son, Hamish (d.1920), lived at 74 West End Lane.

*The Egyptian-style grave of **James Wilson Pasha**.*

83c Vitruvius Wyatt
(d. 16.7.1897)
WC330
Civil Engineer

Named after a Roman philosopher, the 72-year-old Wyatt lived in Goldhurst Terrace and was the victim of a seasonal heat wave in 1897. He had not been well, and one morning failed to answer his wake-up call. Help was summoned, "A builder's clerk was called and he got up a ladder and entered the bedroom by the window, which was open. He found the deceased lying in bed quite dead".

84d Sir Charles Wyndham
(1837–1919)
WE223

(Large stone in the second row, just past the War memorial)
Actor-manager

Born in Liverpool as Charles Culverwell, he was the son of a doctor. Wyndham studied at King's College London and the Royal College of Surgeons, as he originally intended to follow his father into the medical profession. After briefly appearing on the London stage he went to America and worked as an army surgeon during the Civil War, where he saw action at the battles of Chancellorsville, Fredericksburg and Gettysburg. He managed to continue acting in New York where he worked with John Wilkes Booth, the actor who assassinated Abraham Lincoln. Both this and a subsequent engagement ended with Wyndham dismissed for incompetence, and he returned to England. After this inauspicious beginning, he had his first success on the London stage in November 1866 in a musical comedy, *Black Eyed Susan*, and he next appeared with a young Henry Irving in *Idalia*, based on the novel by Ouida. In the summer of 1869 he again sailed for America and after playing leading comedy parts in New York began a 2-year tour with his own company in 1871. He returned to London and became a successful actor-manager at the Criterion Theatre. In the 1890s he put on several plays by Henry Arthur Jones (see **A.47**). In 1899 he built Wyndham's Theatre, which he co-managed with his second wife, Mary Moore.

In 1903 he built the New Theatre (now called the Albery, renamed after Mary Moore's son Sir Bronson Albery, the theatre director, in 1973). Wyndham ran his business from the famous 'yacht room' which doubled as an entertaining space in the evening, meals being sent in from the Criterion Restaurant next door. It was decorated to resemble a cabin, with portholes and lockers. He enjoyed asking people to dinner 'on his yacht' and then seeing their confusion when he told them he kept it moored at Piccadilly Circus.

Wyndham's first wife was Emma Silberrad, the daughter of J Silberrad and grand-daughter of Baron Silberrad of Hesse-Darmstadt. The couple married in 1860 and had a large house – 'Boscombe Lodge' at 45 Finchley Road – where the young Eleanor Farjeon used to attend Christmas parties. Eleanor described her hostess as a "kindly, homely little person". Emma died in 1916 and is buried here. Wyndham was married again the same year, to Mary Moore, the actress he had so often appeared with. In 1917 they moved to 43 York Terrace, Regent's Park, where they were noted for their lavish garden parties. (The house is marked by a blue plaque.) A close friend said "she shielded Sir Charles Wyndham from harm or unhappiness during his last days, when he fell into incapability on the saddest side of that dread disease, aphasia". His worsening condition eventually forced him into retirement.

Wyndham died at York Terrace on January 12, 1919 and was buried here alongside his first wife Emma. His obituary described him as "an actor of unfailing grace and charm, a thoroughly accomplished and secure artist who demonstrated masterly skill" as a theatre manager. The burial service was held in the Cemetery Chapel, followed by a memorial service in St Martin's in the Fields a few days later. Among the many floral tributes, Mary Moore, his long-time companion and business partner, sent a heart-shaped wreath of laurel with her name picked out in white snowdrops.

Mary Moore (1861–1931)
Actress, theatre manager

Also buried with Wyndham is his second wife, the actress Mary Moore. She was born in Islington, the daughter of a Parliamentary agent; the family later moved to Bayswater. Her parents' marriage broke up and her father went bankrupt when she was 12. Mary's new home was in Park Road (bordering Regent's Park) and she married her first husband, the dramatist James Albery (1838–1889) just 3 years later. At the time she was described as "a delightful vision, a slim young girl with chestnut hair". After her marriage she left the stage. Albery was a brilliant and successful playwright, but he was erratic and Mary returned to the stage in 1885 as a sad young wife with an invalid husband and three little children to support. Wyndham gave her a touring part as an understudy out of friendship for Albery, but he did not think she would make it as an actress. However, she amazed him and became his leading lady. They formed one of the most famous partnerships of their time, helped by parts especially written for them by H A Jones (see **A.47**). Albery died in 1889 and she subsequently co-managed both the Wyndham and the New Theatres with Sir Charles. Mary combined an acting career, playing in all of Wyndham's productions, with theatre management. Her speciality was in playing "pretty, but alluring fools – helpless, but not too tiresome and silly". As she kept her good looks right up to the end, she was able to play younger roles than her age. She married Sir Charles in 1916. Her autobiography records that the match was arranged by a mutual friend, Lady Waterlow. Mary felt it was too soon after Emma's death to consider marrying her old friend, but it was pointed out that at 79, Sir Charles wasn't getting any younger! After she died, her son Bronson and Charles's son by his first wife, Howard, took joint control of the theatres. In her will Mary left £178,428 and made specific bequests of valuable jewellery given her by the Tsar and Edward VII.

Sir Charles Wyndham and his second wife Mary Moore in "She Stoops to Conquer".

Section B (see aerial photograph on inside back cover)

In Section B you will find the sons of the newspaper magnate Viscount Rothermere, who like many of the young men buried in the Cemetery were tragically killed in WW I. Also here are Peggy Duff the CND campaigner, Jimmy Cyriax "the father of orthopaedic medicine", and Charles Hengler, the great Victorian circus owner.

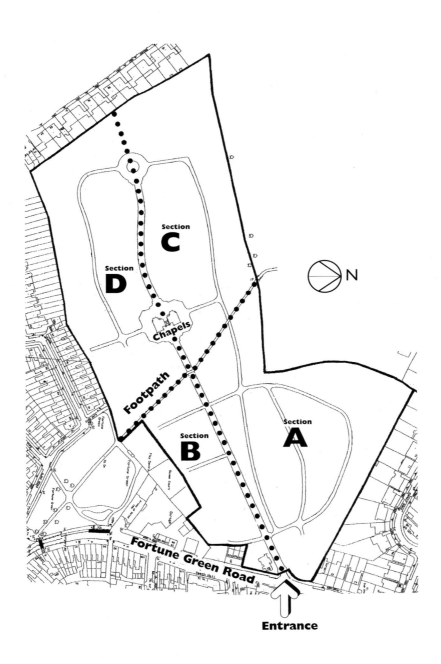

1b Sir Frederick Atterbury

(d. 1919

Q11/24

Controller of HMSO

Atterbury was born in Hampstead and educated at North London Collegiate School for Boys. He qualified as a barrister and won first place in the open competition for the Civil Service in 1872. He held a number of posts in the Inland Revenue and became Controller of HM Stationery Office in 1913. For his civil service work Atterbury was awarded the CB in 1910 and a KCB in 1917. He lived at 2 Upper Terrace, Hampstead Heath.

2a Wilson Barrett

(d. 22.7.1904)

O11/45–46

Actor-manager

Barrett was born in 1846 at Manor House Farm, near Chelmsford, as William Henry, the eldest son of a farmer. He began work as a printer in London but in 1864 he made his first appearance on the stage at the Theatre Royal in Halifax. He tried running his own company, but the results were disastrous, so he joined a stock company in Nottingham to play 'the heavy business'.

In Aberdeen he met Caroline Heath, a starring actress and reader to Queen Victoria, and they married soon after, in July 1866. Acting together in *East Lynne,* the press welcomed him as a newcomer in 1867, although Caroline Heath was the established star. They worked together travelling the country playing in *Faust* and the *Merry Wives of Windsor.* In 1874 Barrett became the lessee and manager of a theatre in Leeds, but after initial success, the theatre burned down. In 1878 he was offered the newly built Grand Theatre in Leeds, and he also took control of the Theatre Royal in Hull. Soon afterwards he also became the manager of the Court Theatre in London, where Caroline played as lead actress. In 1882 the couple moved into 21 North Bank, George Eliot's old house, bordering the Regent's Canal in St Johns Wood. However, Caroline's health began to fail and she withdrew from the stage and died in retirement on 26 July 1887. This may have been the reason Barrett left North Bank at the end of the same year. Earlier, in 1879 Barrett acted in *A Clerical Error,* the first play by Henry Arthur Jones (see **A.47**) to be produced in London. Another long run of 300 days came in 1881 with a second of Jones's plays, *The Silver King,* which *The Times* thought the most successful melodrama ever staged. Barrett starred in this production at the Princess's Theatre, which he was also managing at the time.

The combination of Jones's writing with Barrett's acting and theatre management continued to succeed and they also began to collaborate as playwrights. Barrett wrote a large number of plays, and also published some novels based on his plays. In 1885 Barrett's acting in *Hamlet* even began to rival the popularity of Sir Henry Irving at the Lyceum. Barrett, then aged 38, played

***Wilson Barrett**, actor-manager at age 22.*

Hamlet as a boy of 18. His interpretation was very popular, but for some critics not wholly satisfying. Barrett set a furious pace: "rapid, emotional, hysterical, passionate and restless. . .it was a new Hamlet – of that there is no question, that it was the true Hamlet who shall be bold enough to say?" His brother George appeared as a gravedigger.

However, after this, ticket sales declined and in 1886 Barrett, now in debt, took the company to America, where he made a 6-month profitable tour. Barrett revisited America a further five times between 1890 and 1897, playing 1-month tours, and he also made two visits to Australia in 1898 and 1902. One of his greatest commercial successes was first produced in St Louis – *The Sign of the Cross,* which Barrett both wrote and starred in as the wonderfully named *Magnus Superbus.* It has been suggested that this play was born out of dire financial necessity – if so, it was an inspired creation. Barrett played a Roman who fell in love with Mercia, a young Christian girl, who was thrown to the lions. It was packed with good parts and won the approval of the Church. Gladstone came to see the play many times and even allowed his name to be used to endorse the play on the posters. It was a tremendous success, and Barrett was able to rebuild his fortunes solely on the basis of this one play.

A man of great energy (his *Who's Who* entry lists under 'recreation' the single word – work!) he continued to work as an actor-manager until 1904, when he died after an operation for cancer at a private hospital in London. He left an estate worth over £30,000. Barrett's success perhaps owed more to his personality than to his acting talent. Of average height, on stage he wore shoes with built-in 'lifts', which some critics unkindly referred to as his "golden football boots". The writer of his obituary in *The Times* thought that he was never a great actor, but condescendingly conceded that "he was immensely popular with certain audiences, especially in the provinces, the Colonies and the United States". At the time of his death he lived in Maresfield Gardens. Among the many floral tributes at his funeral were wreaths from Sir Charles Wyndham and the writer Marie Corelli.

3a George Barrett
(1849–1894)
O11/47
Actor
In the next grave is George Barrett, Wilson's brother, who was described as an "excellent low comedian". George, together with his brother Robert Reville and their sister Mary Brunell, were all family members of Wilson Barrett's travelling company.

4a Sidney Arthur Boyd
(d. 2.11.1966)
P5/51
Surgeon, and Mayor of Hampstead
Sidney Boyd was Mayor of Hampstead between 1938 and 1945, and his name is remembered at the large block of flats in West End Lane, built in 1953 to replace the houses hit by a bomb. Born in Bedford, Boyd attended London University, and studied medicine at Charing Cross and London Hospitals, where he qualified as a surgeon in 1902. He moved to Hampstead in 1910 and in WW I he served as a Major with the Mediterranean and Egyptian expeditionary forces, where he was twice mentioned in dispatches. After the war he worked as a lecturer in anatomy at King's College. He later became a consultant surgeon at Hampstead General and several other hospitals. In addition to his busy medical practice he took a very active part in local politics. He was first elected to Hampstead Council in 1922. In addition to being the Mayor for 7 years, he became an Alderman in 1942 and 3 years later was made a freeman of the Borough of Hampstead.

In 1910 he married Violet Evangeline Fox (d.1968, also buried here), and they had a son and three daughters. They lived at various addresses in Hampstead: 33 Belsize Park Gardens (1921), 1 Redington Gardens (1934) and 10 Oakhill Avenue (at the time of his death in 1966).

5a Joseph Brown
(d. 1902)
WB575
Lawyer and author
An eminent barrister who practised at the Bar for 50 years, Brown was involved in a number of celebrated trials, including that of the Royal British Bank directors in 1858. Created CB upon his retirement, he wrote about the problems associated with trial by jury and urged reform. Brown was also an antiquarian and a member of the Geological Society. He died at his home, 54 Avenue Road.

6b Ethelbert Bullinger
(d. 6.6.1913)
R5/8
Religious writer
A writer on the New Testament, he published over seventy works, including *How to Enjoy the Bible*, and two books of hymns. He was ordained in 1861 and held posts in Bermondsey, Norfolk, Notting Hill and other London parishes. He lived at 'Bremgarten', Golders Hill.

7b Sir George Bullock
(d. 1926)
R4/22
Lieutenant-General
Born in India in 1851, the son of the Deputy Commissioner of Berar. Educated at Oxford and Sandhurst, Sir George was a career soldier, serving on campaigns in India, and South Africa, where he was present at the relief of Ladysmith and mentioned in dispatches. From 1902 to 1908 he served in Egypt. In 1912 he was appointed Governor of Bermuda, a post he held until 1917. He was awarded a CB in 1900 and a KCB in 1911.

8b Sir Francis Champneys

(1848 – 1930)

Q9/31

Obstetrician

He was intriguingly described by one obituary as "personally short, virile, and handsome". Francis studied medicine at Bart's and went on to specialise in obstetrics. Probably his greatest achievement was the establishment of the Central Midwives Board. Its first Chairman (1903), he was annually re–elected for 27 years until his death. He was responsible for creating a professional body of skilled midwives in place of the untrained and often unhygienic amateurs. Champneys was also considered to be the finest amateur musician in the medical profession. He died at his home in Nutley, Sussex.

The Champneys family had local connections with Camden. Francis was the brother of Basil Champneys, the noted architect who designed St Luke's Church, the vicarage in Kidderpore Avenue, and his own house 'Hall Oak' at 42 Frognal Lane. Their father, William Weldon Champneys (1807–1875) was born in Camden Town and was Vicar of St Pancras Church (1860–1869), during which time Henry Smart (see **D.61**) was his organist.

9b John Richard Clayton

(1827–1913)

WC557

Stained-glass artist

Born in London, Clayton entered the Royal Academy Schools with sculpture as his specialism. But his first source of income was from illustrating books, chiefly for the Dalziel Brothers and by drawing for the *Illustrated London News*. Clayton designed and produced the figure of St George and the Dragon on top of the memorial in Dean's Yard, Westminster Abbey, in memory of the Westminster boys who died in the Crimean War. He subsequently studied under Richard Cromwell Carpenter, who trained him as a designer of stained glass. In 1855 he was persuaded by Sir Gilbert Scott (for whom he did architectural drawings) to join Alfred Bell, an assistant in Scott's office, and establish the firm of Clayton and Bell.

They set up a small studio in Cardington Street, Euston Square, and after a difficult start due to poor firing of their glass, they produced some of the best contemporary work available, for example at Hanley Castle, Rochester Cathedral and Howsham. Although the company was a huge commercial success, subsequently its glass was later considered to suffer from too much detail and a small colour range. The quality also declined as the firm moved into factory-type production in the 1870s. The west window of King's College Cambridge (1879), believed to be the largest window of modern times, marks the period when standards began to improve, and good examples of their late-1880s and 1890s work can be seen at Ely, Truro and Bath. Nearer to home, Clayton and Bell produced windows in Westminster Abbey (*HMS Captain* window, west aisle 1879); St Michael Cornhill (especially The Magi) and St Paul's Cathedral (St Cecilia, 1907). Locally, their glass can be seen in St Pancras Church and St Augustine's, Kilburn. Alfred Bell (1832–1895) was churchwarden at Hampstead Parish Church for 16 years and is buried in the churchyard there; he gave most of the stained glass to the Church in 1878. Bell was the Gothic enthusiast and specialised in architectural canopy work, while Clayton did figure work and had a strong eye for colour. Unfortunately, in common with many other stained-glass artists, Clayton and Bell rarely signed their work.

Clayton was also skilled in mosaics and was commissioned by Sir Gilbert Scott to decorate the Albert Memorial, inventing a method whereby the tiles were enclosed in glass to protect their colour against decay. But the firm often had to undertake more run–of–the–mill work to make ends meet, which led one member of the Arts Club to comment unkindly "If you accept that kind of order the firm of Clayton and Bell will be known as Satan and Hell!"

Clayton was a friend of Dickens, Ruskin, Rossetti and Holman Hunt. He lived at 'Broomfield House', 11 Fairfax Road for over 40 years, and described himself in the 1891 census as an "artist, painter, sculptor and architect", making no mention of the craft he is best remembered for.

In 1881 the founders' sons John Essex Clayton (d.1904) and John Clement Bell were made junior partners. Twenty years earlier the firm had moved to larger premises at 311 Regent Street, where it remained until the building was taken over by the Polytechnic in 1911. The firm moved from Regent Street to Clifford Street in 1911, but the building was bombed during the Blitz and most of the company records and designs were destroyed. At its peak, Clayton and Bell was the largest and most celebrated firm in the field of stained-glass decoration in the UK, if not the entire world, employing over 300 people – artists, designers, draftsmen, cutters, glaziers, colourmen, apprentices, muralists and decorators. Many eminent stained-glass artists began their training at Clayton and Bell, among them Henry Stacy Marks (see **B.29**), and the firm provided glass for many prominent architects. As evidence of their great success, John Richard Clayton left an estate worth over £74,000 – approximately £3 million at present values. His obituary recorded that in addition to churches too numerous to list outside the capital, the company's work could be found in 43 cathedrals and abbeys in the UK, 50 London churches plus 39 cathedrals and churches in the USA, in addition to examples in countless other buildings all over the world.

The Clayton connection came to an end with the death of John Essex and his father, following the sale of the family interest in the firm. But the company went on trading under John Clement Bell (1860–1944), who was succeeded by his son Reginald Otto Bell (1884–1950) and then his grandson, Michael James Farrar Bell (1911–1993).

10b John Essex Clayton
(d. 1904)
WC563
Artist
Less well known than his father, John Essex joined the company as a junior partner in 1881. He seems to have made little contribution to the family firm, but was a good artist who exhibited five times at the Royal Academy between 1871 and 1885. From 1875 to 1878 John Essex lived with his father at 11 Fairfax Road; by 1885 he was at 145 Fellows Road.

11a James Henry Cyriax
(d. 17.6.1985)
N9/4
Orthopaedic doctor
Jimmy Cyriax, "The father of orthopaedic medicine", was born in 1904. His parents were doctors and after attending University College School and Cambridge, he qualified from St Thomas' Hospital, where he continued to work from 1947 to 1969. His 1947 *Textbook on Orthopaedic Medicine* remains a standard work. He became a member of numerous medical societies in various countries and was Visiting Professor at the University of Rochester, New York, from 1975.

12b Sir William Vibart Dixon
(d. 1930)
R11/21
Sir William was Deputy Clerk to the Justices of the Peace for the West Riding of Yorkshire 1877–1923. During WW I he served on several committees in the West Riding, and was awarded medals for his work with Belgium refugees. He received the OBE in 1918 and the KBE in 1924. He lived locally at 52 Platt's Lane.

13b Peggy Duff
(d. 1981)
S3/25
CND campaigner and St Pancras councillor
The Times obituary described Peggy Duff as "a born campaigner", and a plaque marks her home at 1 Albert Street, Camden Town. She was born in London and educated at Bedford College. A committed left-winger and peace activist, she acted as the General Secretary for CND (the Campaign for Nuclear Disarmament) from 1958 to 1965, and was the organiser of the Aldermaston Peace Marches in the 1960s. Peggy left CND in 1967 to take up a new role as Secretary to the International Confederation for Disarmament and Peace, a post she held until her death. A colleague described her as "chunky, indomitable, sometimes angry, always warm-hearted, joking, organising [or] marching at the head of some demonstration". Peggy wrote a personal account of her campaigning activities entitled *Left, Left, Left.* and also served as a local Councillor in St Pancras (later Camden) for 15 years.

14a Sir John Erichsen
(d. 1896)
WB589
Surgeon to Queen Victoria
Born in Copenhagen, the son of a banker, Erichsen was educated and brought up in England. He studied medicine at UCL, became a member of the Royal College of Surgeons in 1839 and a Fellow in 1845. He was professor of surgery at UCL and became surgeon-extraordinary to Queen Victoria in 1877 (a purely honorary position entailing no duties). His reputation rested less on his practice than on his authorship of *The Science and Art of Surgery*, first published in 1853. This became a standard textbook and during the American Civil War a pirated copy was issued to every medical officer in the Federal Army. Erichsen died at his home in Folkestone.

15a Sir Harold Arthur Fairbank

(1876–1961)

P2/57

Surgeon

This grave is one of a group of 15 individual grave spaces enclosed by low metal railings. They were purchased in 1888 by **Arthur Graeme Ogilvie**, a mining engineer living in Grove End Road, St John's Wood. Presumably his intention was to provide adequate burial space for successive generations of his family.

Sir Harold Fairbank married Florence, one of Arthur Ogilvie's daughters. Harold was an eminent medical man, an orthopaedic surgeon working as a consultant at the Hospital for Sick Children, Great Ormond Street and King's College Hospital. He was awarded the DSO and an OBE, and he held many honorary posts. He lectured widely and contributed articles to journals and textbooks.

Adjacent to the Ogilvie enclosure is a group of 12 graves bought by (later Sir) **George William Agnew** of Primrose Hill. His father, the first baronet, was head of Thomas Agnew and Sons, the fine art dealers in Bond Street, and a member of the publishing company who owned *Punch*. Sir George also helped to run the Bond Street business and was MP for Salford. Like Arthur Ogilvie, Sir George was presumably planning for the future when he bought the group of graves, indeed the two families were friends, but Sir George is not among the Agnews buried here. Those who are include Philip Leslie Agnew (d.1938), who was Sir George's younger brother and managing director of the company. Also here are Sir George's nephew, Major Kenneth Moreland, a distinguished career soldier who died in 1951.

16a Anatole Fistoulari

(d. 21.8.1995)

T/105

(The grave is in the path section by the footpath and the wall, but there is no visible record.)

Conductor of London Philharmonic Orchestra

'Fisty', as he was known to his friends, was born in Kiev in 1907 and had conducted his first concert by the time he was 7. He was taught by his father Gregor, who had studied conducting with Anton Rubinstein and Nikolai Rimsky-Korsakov. Fistoulari conducted throughout Europe and had made his name by his early 20s. He became the principal conductor of the Grand Opéra Russe, and work with Massine's Ballets Russes took him to England, America, Italy and France. At the outbreak of WW II he joined the French Army but was invalided out, and shortly after France was occupied he escaped to London. In 1942 he met and married Anna Mahler, the sculptress daughter of Gustav Mahler. His major achievement was his appointment as principal conductor of the London Philharmonic Orchestra in 1943. In the next year he conducted an average of one concert every 3 days, a pace that proved too much for both the orchestra and the conductor. His contract with the LPO was not renewed, and although he worked as a guest conductor with the LPO and many other orchestras, he never held a principal post again. He made records for Decca and other companies and he also did some film recordings. He continued to tour the world as a guest conductor until his career came to a halt in 1969.

His marriage to Anna Mahler, with whom he had one daughter, came to an end in 1956. In the following year he married the violinist Elizabeth Lockhart. He lived in Redington Road.

17a Ronald Fraser

(1930–1997)

WC688

Actor

The son of a Scottish builder and decorator, Fraser discovered a talent for entertaining when he stood in for a friend as DJ on a local Forces station. He won a scholarship to RADA but left after 18 months. Lack of talent wasn't the problem, rather lack of attention to his studies! He was taken on as dresser to the great actor Sir Donald Wolfit. A few small roles came with the job and in 1953, the part of understudy to Noel Coward in *The Apple Cart* was followed by years of theatre work. Fraser diversified into film and TV in the 1960s and 1970s, and he was soon well placed to pursue his twin enthusiasms of "women and cocktails". His best TV role was probably as Basil 'Badger' Allenby-Johnson in *The Misfit*, a series chronicling the life of an ex-colonial planter. Fraser's mobile and expressive face was his fortune; he could play villains or charmers equally well, but his slightly frivolous manner sometimes detracted from his considerable talent. He married the actress Elizabeth Howe in 1956. They had two daughters and divorced in 1964. Fraser's epitaph draws on Keats's famous sonnet *When I have fears that I may cease to be* for its opening lines.

18a Charles James Fuller
(d. 24.5.1891)
WB573
Priest, founder and Vicar of St Mary's Primrose Hill
This neo-Gothic tomb is the resting place of another of Hampstead's clergy. Fuller was chaplain of the Boys' Home in Regent's Park Road, Primrose Hill, where he held services which were open to locals as well as the inmates. As space was limited and house building was on the increase in the neighbourhood, a temporary church was built in 1867 in Ainger Road to accommodate the rapidly expanding congregation. The Eton Estate then agreed to give some land on the corner of Elsworthy and Fellows Roads as the site for St Mary's. Fuller's future wife, Miss Andre, was a great benefactor to the Church, which was completed in 1872. Designed by William Manning, who was also a member of the congregation, the interior of the Church was originally all red and black, like the outside.

As a keen follower of the Oxford Movement, which promoted a more Catholic interpretation of Christianity, Fuller was unpopular with the authorities, who criticised what they saw as ritualism and popery in the Church services and the decorations. But Fuller's obvious enthusiasm and spirit attracted large crowds to St Mary's, where services were held regularly even though the Bishop of London refused to consecrate the building. A member of the congregation described Fuller as "a priest of high ideals, uncompromising and not always tactful", so perhaps a clash with his superiors was inevitable. In 1877, to avoid the possibility that he might be dismissed, Fuller reluctantly agreed to remove all signs of popery from the building. One of his supporters described what happened: "After Evensong on Advent Sunday came the terrible stripping of the Church, even to removing the crucifix over the pulpit: then began the sorrowful time of no vestments and lights, and for a time, no Sung Mass. It was agony to us all, and Mr Fuller from that time was a broken man".

Fuller carried on with parish life, until eventually a new Bishop of London at long last agreed to consecrate the building. In 1885 Fuller officially became the first vicar of St Mary's, but continued ill-health forced his resignation just 4 years later. In 1891 he died at his home in Primrose Hill Road. Considering the important role Fuller played in establishing St Mary's and its parish, it is surprising that no obituary appeared in the local newspapers: it seems he was a forgotten man. It is worth pointing the irony that his grave is only a short distance away from that of John Kensit (see **B.26**) who fought so strongly against ritualism.

19b Frederick George McGrath Gray
(d. 1941)
Q2/24–25
Owner of the Vale of Health Fair
The Gray family ran an amusement park in Hampstead for about 100 years. Frederick Gray, whose father was a shipbuilder in Bristol, left home as a boy to work for Hancock's Show, where he met his future wife, Elizabeth. The couple left Hancock's and started their own stalls and amusements in South End Green, possibly in the 1880s or 1890s. The opening of Hampstead Heath station in 1860 brought thousands of people to Hampstead. It was estimated that 100,000 Londoners came to the Fair on Bank Holidays in the 1880s. Fred's children worked in the show from an early age and continued to do so as they got married, such that four generations have now been involved.

Fred was quite a character, and claimed he was responsible for the term 'Appy 'Ampstead. However, it seems more likely that the phrase came from a famous music-hall song written by the coster-singer Albert Chevalier in the 1890s. Gray had the first moving-picture show at Hampstead, when he used a hand-turned projector to show pictures of local subjects and a film of Dick Turpin's ride to York. In 1920 Fred bought the Vale of Health Hotel and some adjoining land so that he was able to operate the Fair from that site. Henry Cox was the previous owner and had run a fair there in 1888. The upper floors of the Hotel were used as artists' studios and were occupied during the 1920s by Stanley (later Sir Stanley) Spencer. In the biography by his brother, Gilbert Spencer tells how one Saturday night Stanley found himself locked out and rang the bell. The door was opened by a furious Fred Gray brandishing a revolver. He gave Stanley a tremendous telling-off for disturbing him, before allowing him to climb the endless uncarpeted stairs to bed.

In August 1926 the London evening newspapers reported the capture of a mysterious animal in the Vale of Health ponds. Sightings had been reported of a large black creature with the head of a gorilla and the bark of a dog. Then two surprised anglers said they caught the creature in the pond and brought it to the Hotel where Fred Gray put it into a large tank of water and named it *Happy of Hampstead*. The next day a reporter brought an expert from London Zoo who identified the animal as a young wild seal. How on earth did it get there? Fred told reporters "There is no doubt that there are other big creatures in the pond. We can hear them, and on a fine day, from the hotel veranda, we can see them, through a pair of glasses, sunning themselves. Where they have come from is a mystery." The mystery was not solved until 1968, when one of Fred's grandsons revealed the truth. The Bones, a well known fishing family in King's Lynn, had caught the seal in the Wash and transported it to Hampstead for a lark. Exactly how much Fred Gray was involved is unclear, but he saw it as a splendid joke and to extend the hoax he even told reporters about a second seal which was caught in the pond.

Fred died in his caravan in Redbourne, near St Albans in 1941, aged 79. The Fair was taken over by his three sons, Fred, Alfred and Harry, and their families. Fred Jr, who is buried in another part of the Cemetery (WE70) was known for his generosity, good humour and his black homburg hat. He was made a Freeman of the City of London in 1972 because of his fund-raising. Alfred, who died in 1971, is buried in grave WD72. Various other members of the extended family are also buried in Hampstead, including Frederick James McGrath Gray (d.1983), John Bond (d.1977) and John Franklin Biddall (d.1998). Fred's grand-daughter, who died a month after him, had the unusual name of Alice Hampstead Bond.

20a Charles Green
(d. 1898)
P3/27
Artist

Charles was the better known of the two artist brothers buried here. Born in Well Walk, Hampstead in 1840, he began work in a solicitor's office but by 1859 had abandoned the law to study under J W Whymper, the famous wood engraver. He made his mark as an illustrator and often contributed to the pages of the *Graphic*. His humour was shown in his illustrations of Dickens and very elaborate water-colour drawings, crowded with figures. He used the belfry of nearby St Stephen's Church as the setting for one of his engravings. Charles became an early member of the Royal Institute of Painters in Watercolour when it was housed in Pall Mall and he was heavily involved with its development and the move to Piccadilly.

Charles Green lived in Park Road, Haverstock Hill, but in 1877 he commissioned the architect Batterbury to build a new studio and house in Hampstead Hill Gardens, the aptly if predictably named 'Charlecote', now No.3. Charles shared it with his aunt (an old friend of John Keats), his sister and later his brother Henry. He died there on 1 May, 1898.

Henry Townley Green (d. 1899)

Henry was an artist who exhibited at the Royal Academy but was far less eminent that his younger brother Charles. Born in Islington, he also abandoned a career in the City for one in art. Unlike Charles, who usually chose dramatic, sporting or military subjects for his paintings, Henry favoured rustic themes. The Grove in Highgate featured as a backdrop for many of his works. Henry lived with his brother and died in Hampstead Hospital. As with his brother before him, the funeral service was conducted by the Chaplain to the Royal Institute of Painters in Watercolour.

Charles Green, artist, aged 28 and his brother Henry **Townley Green**, artist, aged 30.

21a H A Vyvyan St George Harmsworth

(d. 12.2.1918)

WB620

Two members of the Harmsworth family, both killed in action in WW I, are remembered here. Vyvyan was the eldest son of Sir Harold Sidney Harmsworth (later Viscount Rothermere), the newspaper proprietor and nephew of Alfred, Baron Northcliffe. Educated at Eton and Oxford, Vyvyan joined the Army a few days after the outbreak of War and became a captain in the Irish Guards. He was wounded several times and awarded the Military Cross. After recuperating from his wounds and trench fever he insisted on returning to his battalion in August 1917. He was wounded for a third and last time at the Battle of Cambrai, and died in hospital in France, aged 24. His body was returned to England and buried in Hampstead in 1918. He was well liked by his colleagues and every year since his death, on his birthday, the Irish Guards have drunk a toast to Captain Vyvyan Harmsworth.

Vere Sidney Tudor Harmsworth

(d. 13.11.1916)

Vere was the second son of Sir Harold Harmsworth. Educated at Dartmouth Naval College, he planned a career in the Navy and became a midshipman in the Royal Navy, but was forced to retired after he was deafened by gunfire. He volunteered for infantry service in the Royal Naval Reserve and saw first action in 1914. Interned for a time in Holland, Vere managed to escape just in time to serve at Gallipoli. He wrote to 'Pater' complaining about the poor rations, and asked for cigarettes and food parcels from Fortnum and Mason's. Not surprisingly, these were well received by Vere and the troops. His father responded to his requests, including one for "a gramophone and the best records, to keep up the men's spirits". From Gallipoli Vere's battalion was sent to France. He was leading an attack on the German trenches at the Battle of Ancre in November 1916 when he was wounded in the throat. Despite this he continued the attack but was wounded again in the shoulder. He sat down and lit a cigarette, and then collected the men around him and led the attack for a third time, but was hit by a shell and killed immediately. Aged only 21, he was buried on the battlefield with his men.

He seemed to have some doubts about living beyond his youth as he wrote in a letter to his uncle St John Harmsworth "Somehow I have never imagined myself as an old man with the infirmities and limitations of old age. At school and in the later years I have tried to imagine myself at 50 or so. I do not seem to fit in. At business in the years to come I shall never be any good...The future...had always been rather vague, far away and unreal. I may have been born just to live my 21 years and then fade away". Sir Harold Harmsworth was devastated by the deaths of two of his three sons. He endowed the Vyvyan Chair of American History at Oxford University and the Vere Chair of Naval History at Cambridge, as a lasting memorial to the boys.

The grave was purchased by Sir William Hesketh Lever (Viscount Leverhulme, founder of Lever Brothers) who lived at 'The Hill', a large house on North End Way. This is interesting because in 1907 Alfred Harmsworth (Lord Northcliffe) lost £151,000 in a libel suit against Lever Brothers. Alfred had personally instructed his reporter, Edgar Wallace, to write a story about the hardships of the poor resulting from Lever's decision to reduce the size, but not the price, of a bar of soap. The story affected the sales of soap and the company were forced to restore the 16-ounce tablet. But they went to court and won their suit, with a large award of damages.

The Rothermere link probably explains why Sir Bertram Lima (see **A.48**), who worked for their newspapers, was buried here a year later. But strangely, his body was later exhumed and re-interred in a corner plot near the gates.

22b Frederick William Hayes

(d. 1918)

R1/16

Landscape painter, illustrator and author

His intended career was architecture, but he abandoned this in favour of landscape painting, particularly scenes of North Wales. A founder of the Liverpool Water Colour Society, he exhibited regularly at the Royal Academy from 1871 onwards. He also wrote and illustrated a number of novels.

23a Charles Frederick Hengler

(d. 28.9.1887)

WC510 (Stone toppled)

Circus proprietor

Second-generation member of a famous dynasty of circus performers and proprietors. Born in 1821 in Cambridge, the son of a well-known rope-walker. As Charles was too tall for tightrope dancing, he became a successful circus proprietor. In the 1840s Charles and his brothers toured the country with their own circus, which was re-formed, with Charles in sole charge, in 1847. Between 1857 and 1868 he built permanent sites in Liverpool (his headquarters for many years), Glasgow, Dublin, Hull, Birmingham and Bristol. In 1871 Charles purchased the Palais Royal in Argyll Street and opened 'Hengler's Cirque' in London's West End on the site of the present Palladium Theatre (opened in 1910).

The 1872 Christmas show of *Jack the Giant Killer* was performed with a cast of 40 children in front of the Prince and Princess of Wales. Charles never performed character parts in the circus, but his skill as a horse trainer was recognised when he was appointed as a riding instructor to the Royal Family. He died suddenly at his home, 'Cambridge House', 27 Fitzjohn's Avenue. Charles was renowned for his professional approach to

The cover of a programme advertising **Charles Hengler**'s *'Grand Cirque', January 1873.*

business matters. He had eleven children, several of whom followed in their father's footsteps. Jenny Louise became a famous equestrienne, Emily and Julia both appeared as juveniles in pantomimes, while Frederick was an equestrian and horse trainer. On Charles's death, Frederick and his brother Albert took over the business.

24b Lt-Col Hugh Marshall Hole

(d. 1941)

Q5/24

Soldier

Educated at Balliol, in 1891 Marshall Hole joined the Rhodesian Civil Service as Secretary to the Administrator, Dr Jameson, who was Cecil Rhodes' right-hand man. Hole served in the Army during the Boer War and WW I. At the end of the war he rejoined the BSA company where he had started in 1890. He wrote numerous books and articles on Rhodesia.

25a Reginald Nevill Jackson

(d. 26.9.1937)

P1/46

Army Officer

Born in Hampstead in 1887, Jackson had a very distinguished career in WW I. In 1917 he was working for the General Staff Intelligence Department as the Liaison Officer with the French Army. For his wartime work he was awarded the DSO, the Croix de Guerre and the Chevalier Légion d'Honneur.

26b John Kensit

(1853–1902)

WC569

Religious activist

Kensit was a man of extreme opinions, and as such provoked extreme responses. He was described by his supporters as "a martyr for the cause of Christ" but was viewed by others as a rabble rouser or delusionist. Kensit was an ardent opponent of the Oxford Movement and objected to ritualism and idolatry in the Church of England. Born and raised in the City of London, he became a publisher and ran a bookshop in Paternoster Row. Founder of The Protestant Truth Society (1889), Kensit was a controversial activist for some 30 years before his final campaign was launched. In 1898, he interrupted the Good Friday service at St Cuthbert, Kensington, by seizing the crucifix. Arrested, charged and found guilty of violent conduct, Kensit successfully appealed against the verdict. An interesting insight is given in the memoir's of C B Cochrane, the theatre manager. He describes how he and Ranger Gull (see **A.40**) concocted a scheme to make some money. "John Kensit was causing a stir with his 'No Popery' campaign. Gull was to write an article against Kensit; when it was

published I was to submit to Kensit a reply – which Gull would also write. The attack, a brilliant slashing piece of work, was published, and I duly called on Kensit in Paternoster Row and offered the answering article, which I read with all the dramatic force I could muster. Kensit was vastly pleased with the article. I asked £50 for it. He gasped at the price; but he badly wanted the manuscript. Gull was waiting in the *Bodega* near by. We cashed the cheque and divided it. It was a fortune to us at that time."

Kensit's views had attracted a degree of public support and he decided to send groups of young men he called his 'Wickliffe Preachers' to spread the Society's word across England. (They took their name from John Wickcliffe or Wycliffe, a religious reformer of the 14th Century.) In August 1902, Kensit put his son John Alfred in charge of the Liverpool 'mission' but when their meetings became increasingly violent, John was bound over not to speak in public in Liverpool for a year.

John Kensit, religious activist.

When he refused to comply, he was sentenced to 3 months in Walton Gaol. On 25 September his father visited the city and gave a lecture at Birkenhead. Kensit was always escorted from such events by the police in case of trouble. Before he could enter the ferry station, he fell to the ground with a deep wound in his face caused by a heavy iron file or chisel, thrown from the crowd, "the missile of an assassin" as his epitaph puts it. It was reported that during his stay in hospital he recovered sufficiently to lead the ward in prayers before finally succumbing to the pneumonia that killed him. John Alfred made a deathbed visit and was later released from prison on compassionate grounds, vowing to continue his father's work. John M'Keever, who threw the chisel, was charged with manslaughter, but acquitted.

After a well-attended service in Liverpool, Kensit's body was taken to the railway station through streets lined with mourners. At the time of his death Kensit lived at the aptly named 'Wickliffe House', 146 Alexandra Road. A funeral service was held in St Mary's Church, Abbey Road, although Kensit had worshipped at Holy Trinity, Kilburn. Immense crowds gathered along the route to the Cemetery and at the graveside itself. Even though the gates of the Cemetery had been closed for 2 hours before the coffin arrived, the crush delayed the burial. Hampstead Council later gave the Protestant Truth Society permission to hold a service at the graveside after the obelisk memorial was unveiled in October 1903, to be followed by a meeting on nearby Fortune Green. One journalist described the funeral as "virtually a monster Protestant demonstration".

Locally, Kensit had attempted to make his point by becoming churchwarden at St Augustine, Kilburn, a leading Anglo-Catholic establishment, but failed. Kensit's campaign was controversial – the entry in the *Dictionary of National Biography* describes him as "a sincere but narrow-minded fanatic", while his obituary in *The Times* was likewise critical of both the man and his work, describing his publications as "hard to defend…even by the most zealous of Protestants. At the last, Mr Kensit's life has been sacrificed in a district which, as having so many indigenous and energetic Protestants, seemed least of all to need his presence". The *Church Times* was kinder, if dismissive: "We confess to having kept a soft spot in our hearts for Mr Kensit. Extravagant, violent and fanatical he was, but we never took him seriously. We regard him rather as a victim of a delusion."

However, Kensit clearly had a large popular following, as the numbers attending his funeral testify. In 1905 the Kensit Memorial College was opened in Finchley, to provide training for the 'Wickliffe Preachers' who continued to travel the country on foot, by rail, and later in a fleet of motor caravans. **John Alfred Kensit** died in 1957 and his place as Secretary of The Protestant Truth Society was taken by his son, **Alfred Latimer Kensit** (d.1992); both are buried here. Like the Society, the preachers and the College are still practising.

27a Edwin Longsden Long
(1829–1891)
WC524
Artist RA

Born in Bath, the son of a hairdresser, Edwin came to London and enrolled at Leigh's School of Art (later Heatherley's), despite objections from his family. However, failing to gain entry to the RA as a student, he returned to Bath where he began work as a portrait painter. In 1853 he married Margaret Aiton, the daughter of a naval surgeon. His situation improved in 1855 when three of his portraits were accepted for the RA exhibition, and commissions followed from wealthy people such as Lord Ebury and Charles Greville.

In 1857 Long studied with fellow artist John 'Spanish' Phillip and made the first of several visits to Spain. He decided to move back to London a year later and produced many paintings influenced by Velazquez and other Spanish masters. Long's work was well researched, and he drew on his visits abroad, such as those to Egypt and Syria in 1874 and 1875. *The Babylonian Marriage Market (*1875), which achieved a saleroom record in 1882 when it sold for £6,615, and *The Egyptian Feast* (1877) both helped consolidate his reputation and Long was elected a full member of the Royal Academy in 1881. His paintings appealed to the taste and religious sentiment of the time and his popularity was increased by the wide circulation of engravings from his pictures, which were particularly suited to black and white reproduction. In addition to his religious and classical paintings, he continued to work very profitably as a portrait painter. For his chief patron, Baroness Burdett-Coutts, he painted her portrait and one of Henry Irving (who sent a wreath to his funeral).

Long moved to 19 Marlborough Hill in 1875, adding a garden studio which he called 'Long's Den' – a pun on his middle name. But this set-up was not ideal. So Long, who was embarking on the most successful period of his career, commissioned the fashionable architect Norman Shaw to design not one, but two grand studio houses. At the time, an artist's home was both a reflection of the man and a setting in which he could entertain and show his work. Long also needed a bigger studio than most, as he produced larger canvases than any other living Academician! One observer noted "it seems no longer possible for a good picture to be produced unless the painter can regard every stroke of his brush from a long distance". The first house, 61 Fitzjohn's Avenue, stood on a large corner plot with its entrance in Netherhall Gardens. Completed in 1880, its official name was 'Kelston' after the Somerset birthplace of his father, but Long called it 'The Labyrinth'. The studio was likened to a church, an illusion reinforced by the presence of a pipe organ. During this time, Long also worked to commission for Agnews of Bond Street (see Agnew above), and his growing status in artistic circles probably explains why he decided to build a second 'Kelston' on land at the end of his garden, using the same architect.

He moved into 42 Netherhall Gardens in 1888. The imposing front door incorporated beaten bronze panels showing knights, possibly crusaders, preparing for war, fighting, and subsequently returning. He painted his last and largest work here, *The Parable of the Sower*, and refused 5000 guineas for it. After his death his widow lived in the house for a further 16 years before it was sold to Sir Edward Elgar and renamed 'Severn House'. It was finally demolished in 1937.

Long died at Netherhall Gardens aged 61, the victim of a 'flu epidemic. The funeral service was held at St Augustine's, Kilburn, but his wife and daughter were so ill they were unable to attend. Long made and signed his will on the day he died. The late addition of a codicil, which dealt with the division of his estate between his children on his widow's death and included a section concerning payment to Long's financial adviser, was contested by Mrs Long. Finally settled in her favour, the decision permanently estranged Mrs Long from her daughter Ethel, who had taken the part of the adviser. His eldest son Maurice died a year later, from injuries sustained in a train crash at Burgos in Spain.

Long left an estate worth over £74,000 but his popularity began to decline soon after his death. An unkind critic once said of him: "Art is long – but Long is not art", possibly a pun on the Latin tag later used as his memorial inscription, *Ars longa, vita brevis*. After the death of his widow, his remaining effects were sold off and *The Parable of the Sower* was auctioned for a mere £131.5.0 in 1908. His reputation has never fully recovered, although today his work again commands high prices and at Christie's one painting recently sold for £100,000. A good selection can be seen at the Russell-Cotes Art Gallery and Museum, Bournemouth.

Edward Longsden Long, artist, by Paul Renouard.

28b Sir Francis Henry Lovell
(d. 28.6.1916)
WC747
Surgeon
Sir Francis was the Chief Medical Officer of Mauritius and a member of the Legislative Council from 1878 to 1893. He was then Surgeon-General in Trinidad and Tobago (1893–1901), later becoming the Dean of the London School of Tropical Medicine. He was knighted in 1900 and lived in Holmdale Road.

29b Henry Stacy Marks
(d. 1898)
P8/36
Artist RA
On New Year's Day 1898 'Marko', as he was known to his friends, was one of the large number of people at Burlington House attending the private view of the Millais Exhibition, but just 8 days later he died at his house, 5 St Edmund's Terrace, Primrose Hill. He was the youngest of four children, and his father Isaac Daniel Marks ran a coach-building firm in Langham Place, which had been established by Henry's grandfather. His talent for drawing showed early, and when he left school he studied heraldry, which his father thought would enable him to paint crests and coats of arms on the carriage doors. At the same time Henry studied at the art school of James Mathew Leigh in Newman Street (one of only two private art schools in London), and in 1852 he was admitted to the Academy Schools. That year Marks also stayed in Paris with his friend, the artist P H Calderon, and studied at the Ecole des Beaux–Arts. Sadly, in his absence the once successful coach-building firm of Marks and Co. failed.

In 1853, much influenced by the pre-Raphaelites, Marks exhibited for the first time at the Royal Academy. Fortunately, his picture *Dogberry* was hung next to Holman Hunt's *Strayed Sheep*, and was bought for £15. Thereafter, Marks was a frequent exhibitor and his work began to sell well. He also found a generous patron in Charles Edward Mudie, the founder of Mudie's Library, who purchased several of Marks' early works, including one with the interesting title of *Toothache in the Middle Ages* (1856). In 1862 Marks moved from Camden Town to Camden Villa, Hill Road, St John's Wood, from which he could go to observe the birds in nearby Regent's Park. With a group of painter friends, including Calderon and G A Storey (see **A.73**), he formed the influential St John's Wood Clique, and on Sunday mornings they would walk along the rural West End Lane to Willesden and Hendon.

To supplement his income, Marks also illustrated books, and did decorative work for the stained-glass makers Clayton and Bell (see **B.9**). Marks designed the proscenium for the Gaiety Theatre, London and the Prince's Theatre, Manchester, and worked on part of the frieze round the outside of the Albert Hall. His work drew praise from Ruskin, who wrote a number of appreciative letters to Marks and even accompanied the family on a visit to Hengler's Circus (see **B.23**). Ruskin particularly liked his studies in natural history, in which Marks specialised at the time. He was a very acute observer of birds, and his skilful drawings of them became very popular.

Between 1874 and 1876 Marks was commissioned by the Duke of Westminster to paint the large friezes at Eaton Hall, Cheshire. This led to commissions in other stately homes. Marks was elected a full member of the Royal Academy in 1878. He worked in both oil and watercolour, and in addition to his studies of birds, he produced excellent landscapes and seascapes of the Suffolk coast. Marks had a good sense of humour and he was popular with his friends and well respected by his fellow artists. He was married twice: first in 1856 to Helen Drysdale (who with their eldest son, Walter, is buried in the next grave) and secondly in 1893 to Mary Harriet Kempe (who is buried with Marks).

30b Alan Moorehead
(1910–1983)

R6/30

Writer CBE, OBE

Born in Australia, Alan Moorehead worked as a journalist (1930–39) and a War correspondent for newspapers in Australia and the *Daily Express* in England (1940–45). After the war he retired from active journalism, settled in Italy for a while, and continued his literary career with such works as *Gallipoli*, which won several awards in 1956 and established his reputation as a major historical writer. He suffered a stroke in 1966 which deprived him of his speech. His wife, Lucy, who had been the women's editor at the *Express*, acted as his typist and he continued to write. His later works included *Darwin and the Beagle* (1969). He was a friend of Ernest Hemingway, the Australian painter Sidney Nolan, and the television tycoon Lord Bernstein. Moorehead lived at 10 Egbert Street, NW1.

31b Samuel Palmer
(d. 1903)

WB691

Partner in Huntley and Palmer biscuit firm

The biscuit firm of Huntley and Palmer's is one of several examples of 19th-century Quaker entrepreneurship, as both the Huntleys and the Palmers were Nonconformists. Thomas Huntley was raised in Reading. His father Joseph sent the 14-year-old to London to be apprenticed to a grocer. Thomas then went to live with and work for his Uncle John, who ran a bakery in Uxbridge High Street. He returned to Reading in 1822 and went into business with his father, opening a biscuit, bakery and sweet shop.

Thomas did the baking and his father kept the books. The shop stood opposite the Crown Hotel, where several coaches stopped each day. Passengers bought biscuits and when they began to ask their own grocers to supply them, the Huntleys were happy to meet the demand. Thomas's brother, a trained ironmonger, developed air-tight boxes which solved the question of how to keep the biscuits fresh. By the late 1830s the firm was well established, producing not just one but several sorts of biscuit and cake. After Joseph retired in 1838 Thomas looked for a new partner, a post filled a few years later by George Palmer, Samuel's brother.

The Palmer family came from Long Sutton, Somerset. Tradition has it that George, by trade a miller and a confectioner, was a passenger on a coach that stopped at the Crown in Reading. George saw the biscuit shop, spoke to Thomas Huntley and so the deal was done. However unlikely this seems, a partnership was struck between the two men which ran for 14 years from 1841.

The company expanded considerably. George was the more active partner, improving the way in which the product was distributed and marketed. 1846 saw the opening of a new factory, and the company could boast over 700 retail outlets in more than 400 towns throughout the United Kingdom just a year later. More family members were recruited to the business; Thomas's son Henry Evans-Huntley and George's two brothers, William Isaac and Samuel Palmer, the last-named also being buried here.

When Thomas Huntley died in 1857 the business passed into the hands of the three Palmer brothers as equal partners, after a cash settlement was made to Henry Evans-Huntley, who wanted to leave the firm. The Reading factory was expanded and over the next 20 years the company's growth was phenomenal. By 1860 it was already the largest biscuit firm in England, producing over 3,200 tons annually.

Samuel declined to move to Reading. He preferred to stay in London, where he was well known in the City. He dealt with the purchase of the ingredients for the company, as well as its London and export trade. He managed to give the business an international standing, moving into new premises in Rood Lane off Fenchurch Street during the reorganisation that followed the death of Thomas Huntley. In 1856 Samuel had married the daughter of one of the company's agents. During their marriage the Palmers ceased to be Quakers, instead turning to the Church of England, whose beliefs were more in tune with the couple's wealth and social standing. Plagued by severe rheumatism for many years before his death, Samuel nonetheless outlasted both his brothers, but his failing health dictated a handover of the London office to his two elder sons in 1887. He formally retired in 1898, following the incorporation of the company. Huntley and Palmer made special biscuits for Scott's Polar expedition. A box found in the tent with the dead explorers containing some of these biscuits was auctioned in September 1999 and bought by Sir Ranulph Fiennes for £3,400.

Samuel Palmer lived in 'Northcourt', a large house at the foot of Fitzjohn's Avenue: the nearby fountain was erected to his memory by members of his family in 1904 and was restored in 1994.

32a Percy Pitt
(d. 23.11.1932)
P4/25
Director of Music Royal Opera House, first Musical Director to BBC

Born in London in 1870, Pitt was educated in France and Germany and his experience of music there helped with his posts as a conductor and composer. He was an organist and piano accompanist at the early Symphony and Promenade concerts at Queen's Hall. In 1902 he was appointed as musical director at Covent Garden and later with the Beecham Opera Company and the British National Opera Company before joining the BBC. He composed a large number of works, including symphonies, chamber music, both vocal and instrumental. He was married to Ivy Margaret, daughter of G H Bruce of Sydney, Australia. In 1928 they lived at 99 Broadhurst Gardens and at the time of his death his address was in Eton Villas.

33a Thomas Gurney Randall
(1842–1928)
WB591
Alderman of Hampstead

Randall was one of ten children, the son of John Randall of Langley, Bucks. As a young boy Thomas lived in Henry Street, St John's Wood, where he worked in a butcher's business together with his brothers Joseph and Henry. He opened his first butcher's shop in England's Lane in 1867, and his name was still over the door 75 years later. Branches followed in Hampstead High Street, Haverstock Hill and King's College Road. The firm held several royal warrants and was well known for the modernity and cleanliness of its shops as well as the quality of the produce stocked. Only the best British meat was sold. It was said that Thomas used to drive to Buckingham Palace to wait upon Queen Victoria for orders. Thomas had his own abattoir behind the England's Lane premises and an 1893 advertisement invited customers to inspect the quality of his stock by "visiting several fields in the parish (where) cattle and sheep belonging to Mr Randall may be seen grazing". Brother Henry (see **A.64**) worked as manager of the England's Lane branch before he opened his own shop at 94 West End Lane. His obituary noted that the family name was "possibly one of the best known in connection with the butchering trade of London".

Thomas Randall lived in England's Lane and Parkhill Road but died, presumably in retirement, in Brighton. He was involved in local government for 48 years as Vestryman and Borough Councillor and, as noted on the headstone, an elected Alderman for 16 years.

34b Sir Boverton Redwood
(d. 19.6.1919)
WC737
Chemist and Engineer

Redwood was born in London and educated at University College School. He entered the laboratory of his father, Theophilus Redwood, of Boverton in Glamorgan, who was Professor of Chemistry to the Pharmaceutical Society for over 40 years. Boverton Redwood's field of expertise was petroleum science, covering every aspect from production and use to transport and distribution. He became a leading authority on petroleum, travelling around the world, chairing numerous committees and publishing books and articles, including the entry in *Encyclopaedia Britannica*. He died at his home, 'The Cloisters,' 18 Avenue Road.

35b William Joseph Goodlake Reeves
(d. 1899)
R1/32

The victim of a cycling accident, William unfortunately lost control of his bicycle as he was riding near Richmond Park. He was thrown off, sustained concussion, and died aged 25.

36b Mary Annesley Voysey
(d. 1905)
Q10/28

Mary was the daughter of the Rev. Charles Voysey and elder sister of the architect Charles Francis Annesley Voysey. She lived at 'Annesley Lodge', 8 Platt's Lane, a house designed for the Reverend by his son. When C F A Voysey was just 12 years old, his father was involved in a very public court case. A descendant of the Wesleys, Mr Voysey continued family tradition by challenging established religious thinking. Scientific discoveries and social reform were causing many to reconsider the position of the established Church and in his *The Sling and The Stone*, Voysey struck at the very foundations of belief by questioning Christ's divinity and the validity of the miracles. Although many sympathised with his view, Voysey was charged with heresy. His trial in 1869 was reported nation-wide. *The Times* even set up a fund to pay for his defence. Despite support from leading members of the Church of England, Voysey was found guilty and told to retract his views, but he refused and was expelled from the Church in 1871. He began to hold services in London and started a movement called the Theistic Church which met in Swallow Street,

Piccadilly, for 30 years. Among his many lay supporters and friends were Darwin, Ruskin and Huxley.

C F A Voysey designed Annesley Lodge in 1895, adopting an L-shaped plan, the house being built close to the back boundaries with no garden space at the rear. In 1906 the architect moved nearby to 14 Briardale Gardens, and his father died 6 years later. Among his recreations in *Who's Who* Rev. Voysey listed "playing with children; all games except chess which was too hard work; billiards at home daily, with or without companions".

37b Sir Ernest Albert Waterlow
(d. 25.10.1919)
P7/47
Landscape artist RA
Ernest Waterlow was born in London in 1850, the only son of Albert Crakell Waterlow, a lithographer. Sir Sydney Hedley Waterlow, Lord Mayor of London in 1872, was his uncle. The family was of French Walloon descent, and their ancestors included the 17th-century landscape painter Antoine Waterlo of Lille. After schooling in England and at Heidelberg, Ernest began his art studies at Ouchy, near Lausanne, continuing them at a school of art in London run by Francis Cary. In 1872 he entered the Royal Academy Schools where he gained the Turner gold medal. His landscapes were frequently exhibited at the Royal Society of Painters in Watercolour, whose President he became from 1897 to 1914. He worked in both watercolour and oil, and his landscapes were popular and admired for their delicacy of colour and atmospheric tone. His picture, *Galway Gossips*, is in the Tate Gallery. Waterlow was knighted in 1903 and became a member of the Royal Academy a year later.

He was married twice, first in 1876 to Mary Margaret Sophia (died 1899), the daughter of Professor Hofmann of Heidelberg; and secondly, in 1909 to Eleanor Marion, the widow of Dr George Sealy. There were two sons and a daughter from the first marriage. From 1892 until his death in 1919 he lived at 1 Maresfield Gardens. South Hampstead High School for Girls acquired the house which was demolished, but his name is commemorated in the school's Waterlow Building of 1988.

38b Rev. Thomas Whitby
(d. 1918)
R3/18
Honorary Canon of Wakefield
Born in Liverpool, Whitby was a vicar in Leeds, Dewsbury, and Sandown, Isle of Wight, before becoming an honorary canon of Wakefield. In *Who Was Who* his recreations include foreign travel and brass rubbings. He lived at 145 Brondesbury Park.

39b Thomas Yeo
(1838–1905)
WC548
Major developer in Hampstead
Probably working together as solicitor-cum-land speculator and builder, Thomas and his father Robert Yeo were responsible for building many houses on the Eton estate at Chalk Farm and Swiss Cottage during the 1850s and 60s. Later Thomas also speculated successfully in West Hampstead. Originally from Derbyshire, Thomas had several local addresses. By 1885 he was living in Priory Road with his wife Helen and their young family, where a close neighbour was the architect Banister Fletcher (see **D.24**) The two families were related by marriage; the Yeo grave notes the death and burial of Thomas' grandson Hugh Banister Fletcher in Australia. The inscription also records the death of 4-year-old Robert, the "darling son" of Helen and Thomas who died in 1888. At the time, wealth did not necessarily protect a family from the all-too-frequent loss of a child, in this case caused by diphtheria. Nor could it prevent the death of a second son, killed in action in WW I.

In 1891 Thomas Yeo purchased 'The Chimes', a large house set in two acres of land at the corner of Quex Road and West End Lane. He lived in the house for a few years, progressively selling off parts of the grounds for building and finally disposing of the building itself about 1899. Described as an old resident and "large property owner in the district", he died at Tunbridge Wells in 1905 and his body was brought back to Hampstead to be interred in the family grave.

Section C (see aerial photograph on back cover)

The north-west corner of the Cemetery includes an area of 'common' graves, where several people, often unrelated, are buried in each grave. It has always been expensive to buy a grave and this was the cheapest form of burial on offer. The right to a headstone was granted to the first person who could afford to put one up. The ground is raised here, apparently, because more earth had to be brought in to create a greater depth for burials.

In Section C you will find the Short Brothers, who designed and built some of the earliest aircraft. The great electrical engineer Ferranti is also here, as is the grave of the fascinating John 'White Fox' Hargrave. The only Nobel prizewinner in the Cemetery is buried here. This section also has a very unusual inscription written in shorthand, and a superb statute by Sir Goscombe John.

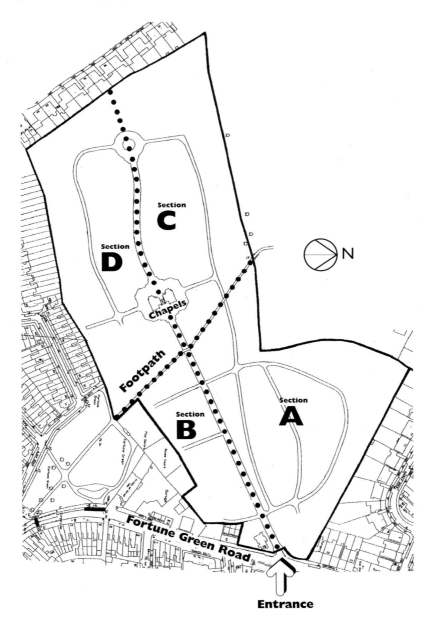

Section C

1b The Civilian War memorial

In WW II a plot was laid aside for the burial of civilians as well as those killed in air raids. The memorial for the civilians who died in Hampstead between 1939 and 1945 contains 50 named and five unknown people. It was agreed that a simple treatment would be most appropriate here, with a rustic paved path leading to the memorial, hedged by floribunda roses and four flowering cherry trees. The Portland stone memorial was to the design of Alderman Milne and erected by Underwoods of Fortune Green Road. The inscription was carved by Mr F Wigzell.

2c George Silvanus Allen

(d. 25.3.1954)
J4/77

Living to the age of 104, Allen is the oldest person we have found in the Cemetery.

3c Charles Bell

(d. 1899)
WC254
Architect

Born in Grantham, Lincolnshire, Bell was a competent architect who designed the Hampstead Cemetery Chapels and Lodge. A competition was held and five anonymous tenders were received – Bell's was entitled 'Resurgam' and he was duly appointed Architect to the Burial Board. The firm of Kendall and Mew came second; Mew's daughter Charlotte, an acclaimed poet, is buried here (see **A.51**). Bell also specified the design of the original Cemetery railings and a coffin rest for each chapel. The cost of building the chapels, entrance gate and lodge was £4843 and the railings £355. Bell's office was in Union Street. He was living at 40 Belsize Park in 1878 when he bought the grave for his 4-year-old daughter Margaret, but by time of his death had moved to Campden Hill Square.

4c Louis Maurice Brousson

(d. 1.1.1930)
WC30
Newspaper editor

A career journalist, Brousson came from a Huguenot family. He worked as an editor of several provincial and London papers, specialising in financial affairs. Brousson wrote for Henry Labouchère's *Truth* for nearly 20 years under the pseudonym of Moses Moss. He lived at 31 Belsize Avenue.

5d Sir William Randal Cremer

(1838–1908)
H9/40
EH Listed.
MP. Nobel Peace Prize winner (1903)

Born in Wiltshire, the son of a coach painter, William started work at age 12 as a pitchboy in a shipyard and was afterwards apprenticed to a carpenter. Arriving in London in 1852 he became interested in politics and trade unionism. Founder and life-long Secretary of the Workmen's Peace Association (1871) he travelled widely to spread its message and in 1889 became the British Secretary of The Inter-Parliamentary Union, whose objective was the abolition of war. Cremer was also Secretary of The International Arbitration League for 37 years and was awarded the Nobel Peace Prize in 1903, donating the greater part of the £7,000 as an endowment to the League. The French awarded him the Légion

Sir William Randall Cremer, Nobel Peace Prizewinner.

d'Honneur, and in 1906 he at first declined a knighthood, but accepted it the following year. The Inter-Parliamentary Union (IPU) is still very active and today involves 130 countries world-wide. They organise exchange visits for MPs to see other countries.

Cremer served five terms as the MP for the Haggerston division of Shoreditch and was elected a member of the St Pancras Vestry in 1884. He died at his home, 11 Lincoln's Inn Fields, and was cremated at Golders Green; his ashes are interred here.

6d Louisa Day
(d. 25.2.1905)
G9/34
(The grave is very difficult to find. Note the row of evergreen trees on the right-hand side of the path. Locate the 6th and 7th trees and then walk up the bank on the left–hand side of the path. From the grave of Reginald George in the front row, Day's grave is 7–8 rows in, lying flat near that of George Seabrook.)
Inscription in shorthand
Louisa and Robert William Day, who lived at 7 Ariel Road, had not been married long when Louisa fell ill with TB. She was confined to bed and passed the time by studying shorthand. She also taught William, who chose a shorthand inscription as a fitting memorial. Part of the inscription reads "In loving memory of Louisa, the dearly loved wife of William Day who fell asleep in Jesus on February 21st 1905, aged 36. Weep not for me my friend so dear; I am not dead but sleeping here. In faith I lie, my grave you see; prepare yourself to follow me."

7c Sebastian Ziani de Ferranti
(1864–1930)
WC241
Electrical engineer
Sebastian was the son of an Italian who became guitarist to King Leopold of Belgium. He moved to England and set up a photographic studio in Liverpool, where Sebastian was born. Sebastian attended St Stanislas' School in Hampstead as a boarder, and later went to St Augustine's at Ramsgate. His early fascination with electricity led him to make his first dynamo at school. He took his degree at UCL, before beginning work for Siemens Brothers in 1881. Ferranti planned a generating plant large enough to supply all of North London, which was built between 1888 and 1890 at Deptford, but on a smaller scale than originally intended. At the time, there was much discussion in the scientific and general press concerning the relative merits of low- and high-tension electrical supply. Ferranti's technology, which was adopted throughout the UK, allowed for the low-loss transmission of electricity using high-voltage alternating current and special transformers. His rival Edison used low-voltage direct current, which prevented transmission of power over any great distance. In 1896 Sebastian founded Ferranti Ltd, one of the UK's largest private companies, which once employed 16,000 workers.

In April 1888 Ferranti married Gertrude Ince, the daughter of his business partner Francis Ince of 17 Fitzjohn's Avenue. The couple lived in Fellows Road, then Chelsea, but later moved to Oldham where the new Ferranti company was based. They had seven children and partly because the young family seemed to suffer recurring coughs and colds, it was suggested that they find a better climate. They returned to London in 1900 and rented 31 Lyndhurst Road. Mrs Ferranti noted that "Hampstead proved an excellent place for schools. There was a very good preparatory school kept by Mr Stallard to which we sent Basil and Vincent. The discipline of the school was splendid and the games very well managed."

But as Ferranti's business was mainly in the north of England they left Hampstead soon after his mother's death in 1906. Sebastian's sons Basil and Vincent both fought in WW I. Vincent served in the Royal Engineers for the entire war and survived, but Basil died from wounds in a Belgian hospital. His body was not brought home – the Hampstead grave contains Sebastian, his wife and parents as well as his 17-year-old daughter Yolanda. Yolanda was diagnosed with appendicitis while staying at the Waldorf Hotel in London, where she was operated on, but died 6 days later. Sebastian was taken ill on a touring holiday round Europe and died in Zurich. His body was brought back to Hampstead for burial with his family.

8b James Forsyth
(1826–1901)
E7/44
Sculptor
James Forsyth and his eldest son James Nesfield Forsyth were both sculptors. A younger son, John Dudley, was a talented worker in stained glass. Forsyth's work is a feature of many churches and cathedrals, notably Worcester. He was associated with William Andrews Nesfield, the leading landscape gardener, and his main patron was the Earl of Dudley, for whom Forsyth did the famous Triton fountain at Witley Court. He lived on Finchley Road, later moving to Kilburn and finally 51 Broadhurst Gardens. James Nesfield made the missing bust which once crowned the Fletcher mausoleum (see **D.24**) and John Dudley designed the stained-glass windows in the consecrated Cemetery Chapel.

9e Frederick William Gaisberg

(1873–1951)

WC293

Pioneer of the recording industry

Born in Washington DC, Fred joined Emile Berliner at the Gramophone Company in 1894. He was sent to London 4 years later to take charge of its newly opened recording studio in Maiden Lane near the Strand. It was here that Francis Barraud (see **A.6**) brought his partly finished painting of Nipper the dog, and the company agreed to purchase the completed work, so giving rise to the HMV trademark.

Fred Gaisberg, pioneer of recording.

Gaisberg made many recordings of music-hall artists such as Dan Leno, Marie Lloyd and Vesta Tilley, and later such famous singers as Melba, Patti, Tetrazzini, Chaliapin and Gigli. But perhaps it was the quality of his 1902 Caruso recordings that laid the foundations for the modern record industry, as up to then the gramophone had not been taken seriously. Fred got his brother William a job at the London company in 1901 and both brothers travelled the world on extended recording tours. Weakened by a gas attack on the Western Front where he had been recording the sounds of an actual battle, William, like so many others, fell victim to the Spanish 'flu epidemic and died in 1918.

Fred stayed with the company until he retired in 1939, remaining a keen judge of musical talent. He snapped up the young conductor John Barbirolli in 1927, and he also helped to launch the career of Yehudi Menuhin. He was instrumental in encouraging his friend Sir Edward Elgar to write his Third Symphony (only recently and controversially completed) and Elgar dedicated his last work *Mina* to Fred.

Fred Gaisberg lived at various addresses in Camden: Gower Street, Rudall Crescent, Fitzjohn's Avenue, Avenue Mansions Finchley Road, and finally 42 Crediton Hill. Coincidentally, he is buried close to both Francis Barraud and Grand Duke Prince Michael; on a tour of Russia in 1900 Fred visited the Duke's palace in St Petersburg, where he gave a demonstration of recording techniques.

10f Sir William Goscombe John

(1860–1952)

WB175

EH Listed.

Sculptor RA

Goscombe John was born in Cardiff, the son of a woodcarver. He studied in Cardiff and London, winning the Royal Academy Gold Medal and Travelling Studentship (1889), then in Paris under Antonin Mercie (1890–1891), where he won the Gold Medal in the Salon (1901). His memorials and bronze statues are to be found all over the world. Nearer to home he made the bronze of Sir Arthur Sullivan for St Paul's Cathedral, the statues of Edward VII and Queen Alexandra flanking the main entrance to the V&A, and the memorials to the Marquis of Salisbury and the Earl of Cromer in Westminster Abbey. He won the Gold Medal of the Royal Society of British Sculptors in 1942 and exhibited annually at the Academy for 63 years. His work is at the Tate Gallery and the National Museum of Wales. Goscombe John was a courteous and affable man, proud of his Welsh nationality and of his own success. The monument here is for his wife, Marthe, who was born in Switzerland. For many years an invalid, she died in 1923. It is based on his work for the memorial erected at Tunbridge Wells to Lady Ellen Webb, who died in 1919. In his later years Goscombe John lived at 24 (now 76a) Greville Road, Kilburn. Here he worked in a studio that was full of plaster casts of celebrated Victorians and Edwardians. During the war the studio suffered bomb damage. Goscombe John died at the house in 1952.

*The life-size bronze by **Goscombe John** in memory of his wife Marthe.*

11c John 'White Fox' Hargrave
(1894–1982)

H12/81A

Artist and writer, founder of the Kibbo Kift (later the Social Credit Party)

In a working life of 70 years John Gordon Hargrave was an artist, illustrator, cartoonist, copywriter, Boy Scout commissioner, inventor, author, and psychic healer. The son of an artist and Quaker, Hargrave grew up in the Lake District, where his life-long love of the countryside was encouraged by his parents. His artistic talent was shown early. By age 12 he was providing line drawings for book illustrations, and he was made chief cartoonist on the *London Evening News* 5 years later. By then the family had moved to Buckinghamshire, where Hargrave had joined the newly formed Boy Scouts. He progressed rapidly through the movement and published a regular series of articles and pamphlets about the values of scouting and open-air life under the name of 'White Fox'. His first book *Lonecraft*, written when he was 19, spread his fame, and his solitary campsite was visited by the sons of King George V. In WW I as a Quaker and a pacifist he served as a sergeant in the Royal Army Medical Corps at Gallipoli and Salonica until he was invalided out with malaria in 1916. His experiences were used to write *The Great War Brings it Home* (1919), in which he argued that civilisation had failed and a programme of outdoor education was needed for regeneration. He found that his views were not accepted by Baden-Powell and other senior Scouts. To put his ideas into action he founded the 'Kibbo Kift' in 1920 to train a body of men and women who would act as catalyst on a corrupt and directionless society and lead it back to health. The name was taken from an old Kentish dialect phrase meaning 'a proof of great strength'. He was promptly expelled from the Scouts.

Hargrave married Ruth Clarke, one of the founders of the movement, and their son Ivan was born in 1921. Hargrave earned a living as a copywriter and layout draftsman in a London advertising agency. In 1923 the head of this firm put him in touch with C H Douglas, a retired Army major who had published books and articles which set out to show that the root of all economic and social problems was caused by a shortage of purchasing power. The solution was the National Dividend, a living income to be paid to every man, woman and child, financed by the national credit. These theories became known as Social Credit. Hargrave saw parallels with his own ideas and tried to persuade the members of the Kibbo Kift to accept Social Credit. A direct challenge to his leadership was made in 1924 by Leslie Paul. Hargrave said that anyone who was not happy had 10 minutes to pack their tents and leave. A minority did so and formed their own organisation, The Woodcraft Folk, which became affiliated with the Co-operative Movement.

Subsequent years saw Hargrave's followers adopt their uniform of a green shirt and take the ideas of Social Credit onto the streets. Green-painted bricks were thrown through the windows of Downing Street. The Green Shirts found themselves attacked by the media and by both political extremes, communists and fascists. Although few in number, they became quite well known and the Advisory Committee included Havelock Ellis, H G Wells and Julian Huxley, while other Kibbo Kift supporters included Compton Mackenzie and Augustus John.

In 1935 their morale was boosted by the victory of the Social Credit Party in Alberta, Canada, but then the outbreak of war halted their actions. Hargrave tried to revive the Kibbo Kift once war was over, but the movement met with little success and in 1951 it was agreed to dissolve the party. Meanwhile Hargrave wrote several best-selling novels. *Summer Time Ends* (1935) received praise from Ezra Pound and John Steinbeck, but Cyril Connolly said "I found this literally unreadable". In 1937 he had also invented a 'moving-map' automatic navigation system for aircraft. Thirty years later he was surprised to discover that a version had been installed in Concorde. Hargrave battled for 9 years to get recognition of his original idea. He succeeded in forcing the Government into a public enquiry in 1976; while they conceded that his invention had been copied and developed to produce the modern instrument, they disallowed any financial award, on a point of technical procedure. It was a crushing disappointment from which he never fully recovered. He was however heartened by the staging of a rock musical about the Kibbo Kift performed at the 1976 Edinburgh Festival and at the Crucible Theatre, Sheffield the following year.

In 1968 Hargrave married his second wife Gwendolyn Gray, an actress whom he met in 1950 and who supported and helped him until his death in 1982. Throughout this time he continued to earn his living through his writing, and his cartoons were regularly seen in *Vanity Fair*. A Kibbo Kift and Green Shirts reunion was held in 1984 at the unveiling of his memorial stone at the Cemetery. Hargrave lived in Rosemary Court, Fortune Green Road.

Section C

12c Charles Hendrick

(d.26.10.1910)

WC228A

Mayor of Hampstead 1906/7

Born in Scotland, Charles Hendrick worked as a linen draper in Belfast and Dublin before travelling to England. Bearing in mind his previous employment, it is surprising to find that he commenced trading in Hampstead as a high-class cook, confectioner and baker, opening shops in England's Lane and the High Street, with a short-lived branch in Belgravia. Like his neighbour Thomas Gurney Randall (see **B.33**), Hendrick was also active in local government, becoming a Vestryman, then Councillor and Mayor. He lived at 41 Parkhill Road and was a life-long supporter of the Temperance Movement.

13f George Samuel Jealous

(1833–1896)

J8/49

Editor of the Hampstead and Highgate Express

Jealous was born in London, of a Lincolnshire family. He started as an apprentice compositor and went on to establish a successful printing business in the Strand. A supporter of the Co-operative Movement, he stood Trustee for one such enterprise and was ruined when it crashed. After a long illness, he again opened a small printing business, this time in the City. Then in 1862, just 2 years after it first began printing, the *Ham & High* was put up for sale. A friend bought it for George Jealous, who remained its editor for 34 years. Jealous tried to make the *Ham & High* the best local paper possible. He was an active radical, interested in the Peace Society, the temperance movement and the education of the poor. Jealous never made any secret of his views, but encouraged all shades of opinion in his paper. He believed that the best check on "possible extravagance, corruption or supineness in the conduct of public business" was to keeping the public informed. Legend has it that he gave his neighbour's son, the young Alfred Harmsworth (later Lord Northcliffe) a small printing set, which started him off down the road to fame and prosperity as a newspaper proprietor. Certainly, Harmsworth worked in the newspaper offices during school holidays and was one of those who sent a wreath to the funeral. The cortège travelled to the Cemetery from Jealous's home in Keats Grove. Most Hampstead businesses shut and among the many mourners were representatives of the Vestry, the local Police and the Fire Brigade.

Jealous was a close friend of the Shaw family (the father was organist at St John's, Church Row, and the son Martin filled the same post at Emmanuel Church, West Hampstead). The Shaws were having money problems, and Jealous apparently decided to help them out by hiring young Martin to teach him to play the piano. Twelve lessons were arranged. Shaw described what happened in his autobiography. "Jealous was already seated on the piano-stool looking thoughtfully at the keyboard. Very impressively I placed his hands in the proper position, and with the utmost solemnity he endeavoured to follow my instructions. He had not what is called a pianist's hands. After about 20 minutes had passed he asked if I would excuse him as he had an unexpected appointment which he must on no account miss." He paid Shaw in advance for all the lessons and left. And every week for the next 3 months a postcard from Jealous arrived at the Shaw residence, cancelling the next lesson. Apparently he'd written them all before he'd even begun! Nor would he allow the Shaws to return the fee.

Jealous lived at 1, Villas on the Heath in the Vale of Health and later in Keats Grove. His carefully chosen epitaph is the first verse of an *In Memoriam* poem which appeared in the local paper. The only clue to the author is the single initial 'P'.

> *Cold is the honest heart and still the pen*
> *Of him who never wrote but what was just,*
> *Who chronicling the deeds of fellowmen*
> *Did not abuse his trust.*

14d James Mansergh

(d. 15.6.1905)

WC221

President of the Institution of Civil Engineers, FRS

Mansergh qualified as an engineer and surveyor. His first job was with a Brazilian railway company, and on his return he helped to establish the first sewage farm in England at Carlisle in 1859. Between 1862 and 1865 he was engaged on the construction of railways in Mid-Wales. With his brother–in–law, Mansergh set up a civil engineering consultancy in Westminster (1866) specialising in drainage and sewage projects. He improved Birmingham's water supply and carried out sewage disposal works for many other towns, including Melbourne, Australia. It was calculated that he worked for at least 360 municipalities or local authorities, wrote some 250 reports and acted as expert witness before 300 public enquiries. Mansergh died at his home 'Lune Lea', 51 Fitzjohn's Avenue.

15b Ernest Pells

(d. 11.7.1910)

E7/50

Interesting epitaph: *In loving memory of Bugler Ernest Henry Pells, Baden Powell Boy Scouts…who was promoted on July 11th 1910 at the early age of 7.*

16b John Samson
(d. 19.4.1925)

E1/45

Engineer, journalist and author

Trained as a civil engineer and architect, Samson worked for the Chilean and Argentinean Governments and introduced 'aerial rope tramways'. He took a great interest in developing South American resources and trade with the UK. He wrote many articles on this and other related topics for the *South American Journal*, of which he was joint editor. Samson lived at 42 Parkhill Road.

17f Albert Eustace Short (1875–1932)
Horace Leonard Short (1872–1917)
WB177, WC269

(Two flat stone-edged rectangular graves with grass in the middle)

Aircraft designers

The three Short brothers, Horace, Albert and Oswald, are famous for their pioneering work in airship and aircraft design. Two of the three are buried here. Their father Samuel was one of six brothers, all apprenticed engineers to Robert Stephenson in Newcastle. Samuel later sank a number of coal shafts and became manager of Little Chilton Colliery in County Durham.

Horace survived childhood meningitis, apparently complicated by hydrocephalus, which left him with an enlarged skull. His many talents in later life were put down to this illness 'swelling' his brain to genius level. In 1890 Horace decided to visit his uncle in Australia. *En route* he met Robert Louis Stevenson in Samoa; was next captured by cannibals, but was spared the pot when they decided to make him their king, perhaps because of his unusual appearance. He escaped and ended up as manager of a silver mine in Mexico. Following their father's death in 1893 which left the family almost penniless, Albert was sent to bring Horace home, but instead, Horace gave him £500 and sent him back to England, following on a year or so later. The family had moved to London, where Albert and Oswald established a balloon works by the railway lines at Battersea. In 1908 the three men joined forces as Short Brothers, Aeronautical Engineers to design and manufacture aeroplanes. Among others, Orville and Wilbur Wright contracted them to build six aircraft. They opened a second factory at Sheppey, later moving to Rochester. A third factory was started at Cardington.

The outbreak of WW I meant an increase in production which by then included bombers and airships – Horace is credited with inventing the name 'blimp', and also a folding-wing seaplane which was used in WW I. He died in 1917 but the company continued to grow steadily, diversifying to build boats and lightweight bodies for London buses. Albert died in Maidstone in 1932. He had a heart attack while at the wheel of his seaplane, although he managed to land it safely.

In 1938 Shorts joined with Harland and Wolff to open a new factory in Belfast. Oswald finally retired in 1943, although he remained Honorary Life President and in 1947 a merger created Short Brothers and Harland Ltd, wholly based in Northern Ireland. The company continued to make aircraft and missiles. In 1989 they were acquired by Bombardier which, over the next ten years, invested large amounts of money to modernise the company. During the 1990s Shorts manufactured component parts for Boeing and Lockheed aircraft.

Horace and Albert Short both lived in Ranulf Road; Oswald died at his home in Haslemere in 1969. In the 1930s he lived in Hampstead at 1 Templewood Gardens, where he had an Amazonian parrot called Laura who refused to talk but sang soprano arias in Portuguese!

18c William Henry Symons
(1854–1917)

WC248

Medical Officer of Health for Bath

Born in Dunster (Somerset) and educated at Taunton, Symons took up the post of analytical chemist to the West London firm of Messrs Idris, which made popular carbonated drinks. He subsequently qualified in medicine at Bart's and decided to specialise in sanitation, working for a while as Medical Officer in the parish of St George the Martyr, Queen Square.

Symons took up his post in Bath in 1896 and proceeded to make many radical changes. He turned his attention to all matters relating to public health, notably reducing infant mortality, curtailing the transmission of disease by the common housefly, improving housing conditions and reducing the spread of TB. He also acted as a Schools' Inspector and City Meteorologist, establishing several accurate weather stations round the city. He died quite suddenly and his body was taken to London for cremation at Golders Green, then burial at Hampstead alongside that of his wife (d.1910) and young son (d.1884). A full memorial service was held in Bath Abbey to coincide with the interment of his ashes at Hampstead. Symons lived for a while in Marylebone.

Section C

19b Robert Underwood
(d. 1897)

E5/46

Monumental sculptor and mason

Born in Hackney, Robert was the founder of a firm of monumental masons which bore his name and traded from two houses opposite the main entrance to the Cemetery. These he named 'Florence' and 'Carrara', presumably to reflect Italian connections with marble and statuary. The business opened about 1879 and many of the memorials in Hampstead Cemetery bear the firm's name. Like his son Richard (see **A.80**), Robert's grave is marked by a very simple gravestone. At the time of his death aged 80, he was living in a modest house in Ash Grove, Cricklewood. (E5/48 is another Underwood grave.)

20b Alfred Young
(d. 14.7.1915)

F2/44

Hampstead policeman shot while attempting to arrest a suspect

Detective Young lived in Benham Place, Hampstead. About 10 pm on 14 July 1915 he accompanied Detective Sergeant Askew to a house in Holly Hill with a warrant to arrest Richard Gorges who had been lodging there for about 6 weeks. It was alleged that Gorges had threatened to shoot any policeman who attempted to arrest him and the police had already visited the house earlier that day and removed a revolver plus a quantity of cartridges. Unfortunately, Gorges usually carried a second gun with him, and when he came face to face with Detective Young on the basement stairs he shot and fatally wounded the 35-year-old policeman.

Gorges, a 42-year-old retired army captain, was tried for murder. The defence alleged that while serving in South Africa he had had a severe attack of sunstroke and repeated headaches ever since. As a result the captain suffered from what his lawyer described as "a condition of grave excitement" whenever he took alcohol. Gorges, backed up by other witnesses, admitted to drinking heavily the day he shot Young and a local doctor testified he was indeed an alcoholic. His lawyer went on to argue that Gorges was angry at discovering the apparent theft of one of his revolvers and in the struggle to disarm him that evening, the second gun went off by accident. Although an unpopular verdict, it was considered that Gorges could not be held responsible for his actions due to the large amount of drink, and he was convicted of the lesser charge of manslaughter. Sentencing him to 12 years the judge commented "manslaughter was a crime of infinite variety, and the variety which the prisoner had committed was near akin to murder".

On the day of Young's funeral large crowds visited Hampstead police station to see the floral tributes on display there. When the hearse started up the Hill at 2 pm the pavement was lined with mourners, and after a brief service at the Wesleyan Church at the corner of Prince Arthur Road (since demolished) it went on to Hampstead Cemetery. Young was laid to rest in the same grave as his wife, who died in 1911. His brief epitaph simply says *Shot whilst in the execution of his duty.*

Section D (see aerial photograph on back cover)

In this section there is a group of men all connected with making music in one way or another. Three graves are next to one another, that of Walter Bache, Sir George MacFarren and Joseph Haydn Parry, with a fourth, Augustus Stroh a short distance away along the main path. There are artists such as Kate Greenaway, architects, the creator of the Golliwogg, a 'Clerk of The Green Cloth', and the man who wrote the lyrics of *The Eton Boating Song*.

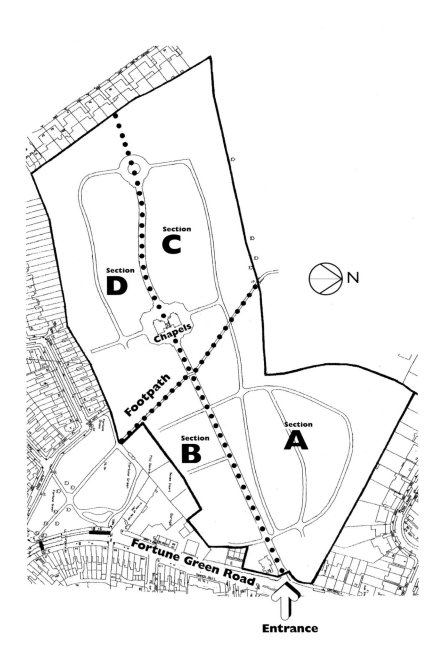

Section D

1a Rev. Edwin Abbott Abbott
(d. 12.10.1926)
D2/96
Religious writer. Headmaster of City of London School

As headmaster (1865–1889) Edwin introduced comparative philology, chemistry and English literature to the school's curriculum and under him it "provided an intellectual training unsurpassed in any other English School". He was the author of many books on religion and lived at Wellside, Well Walk.

2c Arthur Guy A'Deane
(d. 1892)
G12/108

An unusual cause of death. Arthur died aged just 16 at Haileybury College, after an accident playing football.

3c Jane Allen-Olney
(d. 1899)
F5/122
Teacher

Sarah and her sister Rebecca Allen-Olney were both teachers, the headmistresses of Blackheath and South Hampstead schools respectively. Subsequently they started a girls' school at 41 Belsize Park Gardens and in 1890 commissioned E R Robson to build 'The Hall School' in Crossfield Road (their initials can be seen on the façade). The building was sold in 1905, when it became a boys' school. As Jane Allen-Olney was 80 years old when she died, perhaps she was Sarah and Rebecca's mother?

4a Walter Bache
(d. 26.3.1888)
E10/110
Pianist and conductor

Walter Bache is one of several musicians buried in this part of the Cemetery. Born in Birmingham, Walter studied in England, Germany and Italy, where he was taught by Liszt, whose works he helped to popularise when he came back to live in London. His older brother Francis Edward (d.1858) was a pianist and composer. His sister Constance (d.1903), prevented by an accident from making a career as a public performer, was a writer on music and a musical translator, who completed biographies of both her brothers. Walter worked locally as the first paid organist of the Rosslyn Hill Chapel, 1869–71, at an annual salary of £50.

Walter Bache, pianist, conductor and organist at the Rosslyn Hill Chapel.

5c Thomas Spencer Baynes
(d. 1887)
H9/111
Philosopher and editor of Encyclopaedia Britannica

Born in Somerset and educated at Edinburgh and London, Baynes went on to teach and write articles on philosophy and English literature. He was the editor of the *Edinburgh Guardian* until his health broke down: "he had a weak heart and only half a lung", said a colleague. After some time in Somerset, Baynes was appointed examiner in philosophy at London University. He later took the Chair of logic and metaphysics at St Andrews. He was a Shakespeare scholar and wrote the Bard's entry for the *Encyclopaedia Britannica*, on which he worked as Editor from 1873 until his sudden death in 1887.

6c Ernest Walter Hardy Beaton

(d. 24.8.1936)

WC414

Father of Sir Cecil Beaton, photographer, writer and stage designer

There are eight members of the Beaton family buried here. Cecil's grandparents Walter Hardy (d.1904) and Louisa (d.1899) lived at 8 Netherhall Gardens, but later moved to Abbots Langley. Ernest and Ettie Beaton, Cecil's parents, lived at 21 Langland Gardens, where Cecil was born, but moved to the much larger Temple Court, Templewood Avenue when his father's business prospered. Ernest owned a woodwool factory in Bethnal Green and was quite well known as an amateur actor.

Cecil wrote about his Hampstead childhood in his Diaries and described the funerals of both his brother and his mother. Brother Reggie was killed in 1933 when he fell under a train at Piccadilly Circus. The train driver said he thought it wasn't an accident, and this, together with evidence that Reggie's Flying Corps career was in trouble because of eyesight problems, caused the Coroner to bring in a verdict of suicide. His family were devastated.

His mother was buried on a snowy February day: "We stood, a forlorn black family group. The clergyman, with a very red nose, was reading the last prayers...the gravediggers, banded together, moved the coffin towards the grave, then slowly lowered it into the Beaton tomb....We got back into the two motors and, leaving our mother to lie in the cold earth, we returned to our everyday life."

7c Thomas Bowman

(d. 16.4.1905)

WA444

Owner of department store in Camden Town

Thomas and Robert Bowman were sons of a Lakeland farmer. They opened their upholstery business at 108 Camden High Street in 1864, but Robert later resigned, leaving Thomas in sole charge. Mass production in the furniture trade meant prices the middle classes could afford and the business prospered, extending piecemeal into adjoining premises. After a fire in 1893 the site was redeveloped as one shop, and became the largest department store for miles around. Bowmans finally closed in the 1980s.

Also remembered here is Robert Moore Bowman, probably a son. He was a Second Lieutenant in the RFA who was killed in action in WW I and buried in Carnoy, France.

8e Ann Dudin Brown

(1823–1917)

WC660

(In second row behind Rishworth/Potter stone)

Benefactor, Westfield College

Ann was the daughter of a prosperous wharfinger and granary keeper on the Thames. In 1882 she helped to establish Westfield College for women by donating £10,000. Originally based in Maresfield Gardens, it moved to a permanent site in Kidderpore Avenue in 1891. Later benefactions included a contribution to buy land for the site of nearby St Luke's Church and vicarage. Rather than furthering the cause of higher education for women, Ann's gifts seem to have reflected her belief that educated and committed Christian women could be of use to certain evangelical and charitable concerns, notably as missionaries. An only child, Ann apparently had no permanent home after both her parents died in 1855, preferring to live in luxury in suitable hotels. She served on Westfield College Council from 1882 until her death aged 94.

The lettering on her headstone is finely carved and gives a good potted biography. There are pictures of her in *Castle Adamant* (which recounts the history of Westfield College) and in the College itself.

9c John Burlison

(1843–1891)

J5/90

Stained-glass artist

Born in Yorkshire, John Burlison trained with Thomas John Grylls (1845–1913) at the famous firm of Clayton and Bell, stained-glass artists (see **B.9**). Later, Alfred Bell married Burlison's sister Jane. In 1868 Burlison and Grylls founded their own studio at 23 Newman Street and did much of their early work for the architect George Gilbert Scott and his son. Their best-known work is probably the South transept rose window in Westminster Abbey. Like their mentors, Burlison and Grylls did not sign their glass.

Between 1884 and 1898 Grylls lived at Burgh House, Hampstead where he held popular musical evenings. At the time of his death, John Burlison was living in Grove End House, Highgate Road. His gravestone has weathered badly and there is no visible inscription but appropriately enough, he is commemorated by a Clayton and Bell stained-glass window in St John's, Hampstead where his father, John Burlison the elder, is buried in the churchyard.

Section D

10b Rosa Nouchette Carey
(1840–1909)
F2/122 *(No grave visible)*
Novelist

Born in London, one of the eight children of a shipbroker, Rosa wrote poems and stories to amuse her brothers and sisters, which is how her first book *Nellie's Memories* was conceived. Upwards of 40 more novels followed as well as short stories, many appearing in the *Girls Own Paper* where Rosa was on the staff. A woman with deep religious convictions, Rosa believed a woman's place was in the home; *The Lady* magazine described her work as "immaculately pure, and very high in tone". *The Times* noted in her obituary "she wrote admirable books for girls", but a less charitable critic has since described her characters as "lacking any redeeming vice"! However, she did write a few racier titles under her pen-name of *Le Voleur*. Rosa lived at 57 Alexandra Road before moving to Putney, where she died at her home, Sandilands, in Keswick Road. She left an estate worth nearly £11,000.

11a George James Charlton
(1899–1979)
D5/70B *(No grave visible)*
Artist

Charlton served in WW I and went on to develop a career in the art world. He was a member of staff at the Slade where he had won scholarships as a pupil. He also taught locally at Willesden School of Art (1949–1959). The Tate Gallery has examples of his work. George lived at 40 New End Square, where a frequent visitor was Stanley Spencer, who painted a portrait of Charlton's wife.

12e Ewan Christian
(1814–1895)
L9/89-90
Architect

Ewan was descended from the same family as Fletcher Christian of *Mutiny on the Bounty* fame. Born in Marylebone in 1814, he studied first under architect Matthew Habershon and later with John Brown of Norwich. In 1842 he set up on his own at 44 Bloomsbury Square, which doubled as both home and office. After his marriage to Annie Bentham (a relation of Jeremy Bentham) the couple moved to 6 Eton Villas (1851) and then 3 Oak Villas, Haverstock Hill (1858). They attended St John's Chapel Downshire Hill, where for more than 35 years Ewan was a Sunday School teacher and Superintendent. He also worshipped at St Stephen's Rosslyn Hill.

President of RIBA (1884–1886) and architect to the Ecclesiastical Commissioners from 1851 to his death, Christian was responsible for over 2000 works, of which some 1300 were restorations. His most famous building is the National Portrait Gallery in London (begun in 1890 and completed posthumously in a style not truly his own, a continuation of the classical National Gallery next door). His many houses include Glyndebourne, where he encased the old building in Tudor Gothic brickwork and added bay windows (1876).

Ewan was a reserved and severe man, an Evangelical Christian with a strong sense of duty. He was a very successful architect, but there are mixed opinions over the quality of his work. Some people praise it for its simplicity of design, but others feel that his original buildings, although competent, are not exciting. His obituary in *Building News* tends to the latter view, describing Ewan as "safe...in no sense a heaven-born genius". His masterpieces may be few and far between, but they do exist. One such was St Mark's Church, Leicester (1872) and locally there is 'Thwaitehead', at 50 Well Walk (1881–2), the large house he built for himself and named after his mother's birthplace in Lancashire. His initials are on the weathervane and the broad band round its wall was originally inscribed with biblical texts. It is said that Christian rejected some designs by Sir Gilbert Scott Jr, and when Scott, who suffered certain mental problems, heard the news, he went to see Christian and urinated on the doorstep of Thwaitehead, presumably to show his opinion of its owner.

In February 1895 Christian caught a chill when surveying a church in Holloway and died a week later.

13a Thomas Spencer Cobbold
(1828–1886)
E1/86-87
Geologist

Three generations of Cobbolds are listed in the *Dictionary of National Biography*: Elizabeth (1767–1824) and her son Richard (1797–1877), both writers, and Richard's son Thomas, a skilled geologist and helminthologist, or specialist in the study of parasitic worms. Born in Ipswich, Thomas studied at Edinburgh and moved to London in 1856. Working at St Mary's Hospital, the Middlesex and the Royal Veterinary Hospital, he lectured on botany, zoology, comparative anatomy and later became a consultant. He was also appointed Professor of Geology at the British Museum. Thomas wrote many books and articles, among them the curiously entitled *Is the Giraffe Provided With more than Two Horns?* He lived in Portsdown Road, Paddington.

14a **Alfred Felix Corroux**
(d. 1882)

WC445

Clerk of the Board of Green Cloth

Alfred joined the Royal Household about 1830 as an apprentice in the kitchens. He worked his way up as larderer, yeoman of the kitchen, and third master cook. Then he moved through the administrative ranks to become the First Clerk of the Green Cloth. The Board of Green Cloth is believed to take its name from the green covering of the table where it originally transacted its business. It was mainly responsible for the work and finances of the Lord Steward's department which dealt with the 'below stairs' running of the Royal Household, including the purchase and serving of food. It was also responsible for the 'Liberty of the Verge', an area within 12 miles of the Palace of Westminster, where it provided a Coroner's Court and had the power to try all acts of treason, murder and felonies committed within its boundaries. It also licensed public houses and still exists today as a licensing authority. Corroux was based at St James's Palace. He retired in 1888 and his son George followed in his footsteps.

15e **William J. Cory**
(1823–1892)

L4/91

Teacher and poet

Although he was a brilliant writer of Latin verse, Cory is perhaps best known as the lyricist of the Eton Boating Song. Born William Johnson in Torrington, Devon, he was educated at Eton and King's College Cambridge. He returned to teach at Eton and was probably the most liberal and outstanding master during his 27 years at the school (1845–72), where he attempted to widen the classical curriculum to include science, history and philosophy. He left the school quite suddenly at Easter 1872 and assumed the name of Cory a few months later. No definite reason is given for his departure, but it is generally believed that the Headmaster acted after seeing an indiscreet letter Cory had written to one of the pupils. His name was removed from the title pages of two Latin textbooks he had written while at Eton.

Aged 55, Cory left Devon in poor health and moved to Madeira. There he met and married Rosa Guille. The couple had a son and after returning to England in 1882, they settled in Hampstead. Cory was still recognised as a gifted teacher and he taught classics to young ladies, living first in Cannon Place and then 8 Pilgrims Lane, where he died in 1892.

16a **Henry Perry Cotton**
(d. 1881)

WA394

Landowner

Henry was the black sheep of the Powell Cotton family, whose home was Quex Park in Kent. They owned land at the Kilburn end of West End Lane and in Cricklewood, bordering Shoot Up Hill and Edgware Road. This explains the many 'Kentish' street names in the area, from Quex and Acol in the South, to Ebbsfleet and Fordwych in the North.

Henry's first wife was the daughter of his regimental commander in India but the marriage was unhappy, and Henry set up home with his mistress Charlotte, who is also buried here. They were finally able to marry when Henry's wife died in 1868. The couple couldn't or wouldn't live at Quex Park and spent much of their married life in Kingsgate Lodge, a large house on Shoot Up Hill, south of Mill Lane. Henry was so happy here that it was his specific wish to be buried at Hampstead and not in the family vault in Kent. Coincidentally, he had earlier tried to sell some of his land to the parish as the site for the new Hampstead Cemetery.

Henry Perry Cotton, *local landowner.*

Section D

17a Alfred Culverhouse

(d. 1888)

WA391

Local developer

Proof of the saying "where there's muck, there's brass", the Culverhouse family appear to have made money by contracting with the local authority for rubbish removal and watering the main roads in summer in the days before they were paved, in order to keep the dust down. They were also Hampstead farmers, owned brickfields and bought pieces of land which they tried to build on or sold on for profit. John Culverhouse, Alfred's father, acquired West End Green in 1871 and later tried to develop it, finally agreeing to sell it as an open space. He was also part-owner of Fortune Green which again he attempted to build on. His home was the substantial Burcott House, Willesden Lane, while Alfred lived in Willes Road, Kentish Town.

There are several other Culverhouse graves in the Cemetery, but it is not possible to say whether they were all members of the same family.

18a James Bridge Davidson

(d. 8.10.1885)

E1/116

Writer

He was the son of James Davidson, the Devon antiquary and bibliographer, who lived at Secktor (modern spelling Sector), near Axminster. At the time of his death James Bridge lived at 1 Raymond Buildings, Gray's Inn. Previously he had occupied rooms in Old Square, Lincoln's Inn and hence his gravestone is inscribed "of Secktor, Axminster and Lincoln's Inn". The DNB says "a man cautious and reserved like his father". He published numerous articles.

19a Henry James Dickers

(d. 28.4.1919)

D12/104

Owner of Avenue Farm, Cricklewood

Henry Dickers (wrongly called 'Daddy Dickens') was the owner of Avenue Farm, whose fields adjoined the northern boundary of the Cemetery. Locals who recall Dickers describe him as permanently bad-tempered, which is hardly fair. What they remember is being driven off by Henry and his wife Sarah Ann after trespassing on his land and chasing his livestock! At one point he used a flock of geese to guard the farm entrance on Cricklewood Lane.

Dickers was churchwarden of All Saints' Church Childs Hill from 1880 to 1903 and he also served as a member of the District Council and as a Guardian of the Poor. Some of the farm land was sold for building after he and his wife died within a few weeks of each other in 1919, but the farmhouse itself was only demolished to make way for the aptly named 'Farm Avenue' in December 1931.

20a Sir Francis Bernard Dicksee

(1853–1928)

C10/91–93

Artist, KCVO 1917, 12th President of the RA 1924–1928

Frank Dicksee came from an artistic family and studied at the Royal Academy Schools. His paintings had a romantic, sentimental or melodramatic theme and for a while he was a fashionable portrait painter, especially popular with female sitters. He was described as "courteous, warm-hearted and courageous in his convictions".

Frank was aged 71 when he was elected PRA, beating the architect Sir Reginald Blomfield in the second ballot. As President, Dicksee soon had a difficult problem to deal with. The artist Charles Sims had painted George V, but the King informed Dicksee that he was not happy about the finished portrait, which although a splendidly flamboyant composition, had the legs of a ballet dancer! Sims received his fee of 250 guineas and it was agreed that the picture would be destroyed. However, Sims subsequently exhibited it in New York in 1925. The RA paid a further 750 guineas and took possession of it 'unreservedly'. The official records are silent about its final fate, but it was rumoured that at first the head was cut from the rest of the canvas and later all of the portrait was burned in the boilerhouse of the RA. The Council of the RA arranged for a new portrait by Sir Arthur Cope which was approved, and considered by Queen Mary to be the best likeness of George V.

A bronze bust of **Sir Frank Dicksee** *PRA, by his neighbour, Sir William Goscombe John.*

In 1928 Dicksee died of complications following a serious operation and his funeral service was held at Westminster Abbey; the King sent a representative and Sir Frank's neighbour, Sir William Goscombe John (see **C.10**) was among the many mourners at Hampstead Cemetery. Goscombe John also did a bronze bust of Sir Frank for the Royal Academy in 1907. Dicksee lived at 'Greville House', 3 Greville Place, off the Edgware Road, and left an estate worth £37,905.

21a George Haycock Dodgson
(1811–1880)
E3/132
Artist
Born in Liverpool, Dodgson was first apprenticed as a draftsman to George Stephenson, the railway engineer. But due to ill health, he gave up this work and turned to painting and moved to London. Here Dodgson was successful, producing drawings for the *Illustrated London News* and other publications, and he exhibited at the Royal Academy (1838–1850). He was a frequent visitor to Hampstead as one of a group of painters who formed a club that met at the Bull and Bush, North End to use its skittle alley. Dodgson lived at 28 Clifton Hill.

22a John Dowson
(d. 24.8.1881)
E9/99
Orientalist
This is a *memorial* to John Dowson, who is buried in Worthing Cemetery. He studied Eastern Languages and in 1855 was appointed Professor of Hindustani at both University College London and the Staff College, Sandhurst. A meticulous researcher, his chief work was an 8-volume *History of India* as told by its own historians during the Mohammedan period, which laid the foundation for much subsequent study. The grave was bought by the Rev. Robert Crucifix of Boundary Road for the burial of John Dowson's fourth son.

23c Charles Eley
(d. 1902)
WB493
Co-founder of Eley's gun cartridge manufacturers
In 1841 Charles' father was killed by an explosion in his factory in Bond Street, and the firm passed to his three sons, William, Charles and Henry. William moved to Woodbine Cottage in 1854, a Regency villa set in grounds which stood roughly on the site of Lyncroft Gardens, off Fortune Green Road. His widowed mother came too but died of cholera the same year. No other deaths were recorded in the neighbourhood, but the unfortunate Mrs Eley was in the habit of having a bottle of water delivered from a pump near Golden Square, Soho. This important fact helped Dr John Snow prove that cholera was spread by water, in this case from the Soho pump. William Eley set up a small factory near Woodbine Cottage, probably for research purposes rather than manufacture. Charles and his wife Elizabeth took over from William, finally leaving Woodbine Cottage about 1872. The couple later moved to 59 Finchley Road and Charles was made Chairman of Eley Brothers Ltd in 1888, a post he held until his death. The company was later taken over by ICI, but the name of Eley still survives on the shot-gun cartridges.

24e Banister Fletcher
(1833–1899)
A1
EH Listed.
Professor of Architecture, FRIBA
The grave is an elaborate mausoleum by his eldest son, Sir Banister Flight Fletcher, made from Portland stone. The family arms are carved on the central pedestal, which was originally topped by a bronze bust of Banister Fletcher made by local sculptor James Nesfield Forsyth (see **C.8**). The two life-sized figures seated on the steps represent Faith and Fortitude. Although a large number of the family are commemorated here, the vault below is the resting place for just eight members of the Fletcher family, including Banister, his wife and four of their children.

Judging by the inscriptions detailing their honours and achievements, both father and eldest son were incredibly talented and very hard workers. They were successful architects who together produced *A History of Architecture on the Comparative Method* (1896), still considered a vital reference work. The family lived in 'Anglebay', a large house (now demolished) on the corner of Woodchurch Road and West End Lane, which may have been built to Banister's own design. He designed several other distinctive houses in nearby roads, for example 82 Compayne Gardens and 5 Cleve Road. In addition to holding many professional posts, Banister Fletcher was elected Liberal MP for Northwest Wiltshire, 1885–6. He was also a JP, and there is a story that a man he had convicted later vandalised the grave by knocking off the bust as an act of revenge against what he saw as an unjust sentence.

Sir Banister Flight Fletcher (1866–1953)
Architect, Barrister at Law
Banister Flight was articled to his father, and studied architectural design at the RA Schools and in Paris, winning many prizes during his years as a student. In 1889 he entered into partnership with his father and brother Herbert Phillips. Most of his work was done under the name of 'Banister Fletcher and Sons'. Banister Flight greatly expanded the 100-page architectural textbook which he had written with his father. This firmly

established his name: not many men can have made such a wide and solid reputation with a single book.

Banister Flight was called to the Bar in 1908 and knighted in 1919. He was a member of numerous professional institutions and committees, serving as President of RIBA from 1929 to 1931. Locally, he designed the International College at the corner of Lymington Road and Finchley Road. He was twice married; his first wife Alice Maude Mary Bretherton was a star pupil at Cheltenham and an active member of the Woman's National Liberal Foundation. She died in 1932, and is also buried here.

Herbert Phillips Fletcher (1872–1917)

Herbert followed his father and brother as an architect. He was a skilled student, gaining the highest examination diplomas at the Institute of British Architects, the Surveyors' Institute and the Institution of Civil Engineers. After qualifying, he was called to the Bar at Middle Temple, and became a partner in the family firm of architects. When war broke out he joined the Royal Flying Corps and from March 1915 to February 1916 he was lent to the French Navy as senior military observer for reconnaissance work in seaplanes from Aden to Gallipoli. For this work he was awarded the Croix de Guerre three times, and he also won the DSO. He died in August 1917 and is buried here in the family grave.

25a Dr Walter Flight

(d. 4.11.1885)

C10/155

Mineralogist

Dr Flight studied in London and Germany and lived at 4 Wildwood Terrace, North End. His son Claude (d.1955) worked as a farmer and beekeeper before WW I, but later studied art, specialising in linocut prints and water-colours and developing a highly individual style of both painting and design.

26a Leonard Upcott Gill

(d. 1919)

C11/109

Founder of Exchange and Mart

Gill joined the family publishing business and after working on several papers was made editor of *The Bazaar, Exchange and Mart*. Originally a small ads sheet, it expanded to two and then three issues a week. Articles were added on country life, gardening, mechanics and household interests, with a questions and answers page. Gill lived at 65 Minster Road.

27c Kate Greenaway

(1846–1901)

G3/120

(Quite difficult to find. Three rows to the right of Lister and then five graves back from Strickland, near a tree)

Painter, illustrator and author

Catherine, more commonly known as Kate, Greenaway was born in London the daughter of a wood engraver, and grew up at a farm in Rolleston, Notts. She studied art at Heatherley's and the Slade and began exhibiting in 1868. The artist Henry Stacy Marks (see **B.29**) was a friend and encouraged her work. Beginning with Valentine and Christmas-card illustrations, she wrote many children's books. Her first success was *Under the Window, Pictures and Rhymes for Children* (1871), which sold over 100,000 copies. In 1883 the first *Kate Greenaway Almanack* was published and her drawings had a powerful influence on children's clothes throughout Europe and America. One of her greatest admirers was Arthur Liberty, and his shop featured clothing based on her drawings. After her death Liberty was the honorary treasurer of her memorial fund, which was used for a Kate Greenaway cot at the Hospital for Sick Children, Great Ormond Street. Today she is best known as an illustrator, especially of children dressed in stylised costumes. Memories of the rural and old-fashioned lifestyle in Rolleston helped shape these images, and Kate bought clothes from this and other villages to use as studies for her work. She also designed beautiful bookplates and her work was much admired by John Ruskin.

Kate Greenaway, writer and illustrator of children's books.

In 1885 Kate commissioned Norman Shaw to build a house at 39 Frognal where she lived with her parents, John and Elizabeth, for the rest of her life. Marked by a blue plaque, the house is tile-hung in the style of a Surrey Weald cottage with a studio across the top floor. Locally, her name is remembered in Greenaway Gardens (Hampstead) and Greenaway House (Boundary Road) and nationally by a medal awarded annually to the best illustrator of children's books. Despite the great popularity of her work, Kate was a shy person who shrank from publicity.

In 1899 Kate was diagnosed as having breast cancer. The next year she visited friends in Newhaven and in the visitors' book wrote a four-line verse, completing the work on her return to London. Her epitaph *Heaven's blue skies may shine above my head, while you stand there – and say that I am dead!* forms part of that longer poem. Kate was cremated at Woking and after a simple service, her ashes were interred in her parents' grave at Hampstead Cemetery.

28a Henry Andrade Harben (d. 1910)
Guy Philip Harben (d. 1949)
WA 389

Chairmen of the Prudential Assurance Company

Henry Andrade Harben was the son of Sir Henry Harben. In 1852 Sir Henry joined the Prudential, a small company which began in Blackfriars in 1848. He made the radical suggestion that they should start a scheme of life assurance for the working classes. This was very successful and he also introduced scientific principles to life assurance. Harben became director of the company in 1873 and was made Chairman in 1905, having received a knighthood on Queen Victoria's diamond jubilee in June 1897. He gave large sums of money for charitable work and built a Convalescent Home for Working Men in Littlehampton at a cost of £50,000. For 50 years Sir Henry's London home was Seaford Lodge in Fellows Road, Hampstead. He played a major part in local affairs as Chairman of the Vestry and as Hampstead's representative on the LCC from 1889 to 1894. Then in 1900 he became the first mayor of Hampstead. In 1911 he died at his country house near Horsham and was buried in Kensal Green Cemetery. His only son was Henry Andrade Harben (1849–1910), who had joined the firm and succeeded him as chairman of the Prudential. In 1885 he was living at 68 Fellows Road.

Guy Philip Harben was the son of Henry Andrade, and Sir Henry's grandson. Educated at Rugby, Guy studied at the Slade School of Art. He worked as an artist in Italy where he was the Board of Trade Commissioner in 1915. During the War he was a special attaché at the embassy in Rome and he was awarded the OBE in 1917. At the end of the war he followed in the family footsteps and joined the Prudential, becoming Deputy Chairman from 1936 to 1948. In *Who's Who* he gave his recreations as orchid growing and fly-fishing.

29c George Holford
(d. 20.5.1904)
WB465

Old Hampstead landowning family

The family name is remembered in Holford Road, which cuts through the grounds of what was once Holford House near the Whitestone Pond. The Holfords were actively involved in Hampstead's social, administrative, educational, charitable and religious life. George was part of the fourth generation of Holfords, the son of Charles and his second wife Mary Ann, and a barrister by profession. His wife and daughter are also here, while other family members are buried in the churchyard at Hampstead Parish Church.

30c Commander A T Johnstone
(d. 1916)
WC437

RN, killed at Battle of Jutland

The Battle of Jutland took place on 31 May 1916, off the west coast of Denmark. It was the only major fleet action of WW I and was the largest naval battle of all time. More than 330 British sailors were killed and six cruisers were sunk, among them *HMS Defence*. The battle cruiser *Invincible* had disabled two German light cruisers, and *Defence* and *Warrior* from the First Cruiser Squadron were attempting to sink them when they were hammered by fire from the German battleships. *Defence* was blown up and *Warrior* was set on fire but managed to escape. Johnstone had entered the navy as a cadet in 1896 and reached the rank of Commander. He had served on *HMS Defence* as its gunnery officer since April 1915.

Section D

31a Sir John Scott Keltie
(d. 1927)
C12/85
Geographer and writer
Keltie was the Librarian (1885–1892) and Secretary (1892-1915) of the Royal Geographical Society, who started the *Geographical Journal*. He wrote widely on geographical and scientific matters. Today his epitaph seems a trifle extravagant in its claims: *His name has remained in the eyes of all men, the Incarnation of geography.* Knighted in 1918, Sir John lived in Broadhurst Gardens, later moving to 88 Brondesbury Road.

32c Ralph Winnington Leftwiche
(d. 25.3. 1919)
WC631
Raised Shakespeare Memorial in Southwark Cathedral
The memorial in Southwark Cathedral was designed by Henry McCarthy (1912), and a service is held there each year to mark Shakespeare's birthday. The memorial shows a reclining figure of the playwright, with the buildings of Southwark carved as a relief behind him. Shakespeare's youngest brother is buried in the cathedral and many of his friends and colleagues worshipped there, for there were five theatres nearby, including the Globe. Dr Leftwiche's epitaph records that the memorial was due to his efforts and researches; he acted as Secretary of the Committee to raise the necessary funds – £650. At the time he was living at 125 Kennington Road.

33a Charlotte Letts
(d. 26.3.1886)
E1/110
Widow of Rev. John Letts, Rector of St Olave's, Hart Street, City of London
St Olave's is the church where Samuel Pepys was buried. A tablet inside the Church recorded the fact that the Rev. Letts's daughter had a miraculous escape when she survived a fall from the top floor of the rectory onto the basement's paving stones.

34c Lord Joseph Lister
(1827–1912)
WA432
EH Listed.
Pioneer of antiseptic surgery
Lister was the pioneer of antiseptic surgery, using carbolic acid to kill germs. Today's 'Listerine' was named after him. Among many important posts, he was Serjeant Surgeon to Queen Victoria. Lister's father was a wine merchant in London, but the family home was Upton House, a large mansion in the village of that name in Essex (long since absorbed into East London, where it borders West Ham). Here Lister was born and brought up to follow his parents' Quaker beliefs. After a BA at University College London, he moved on to its Medical School (1848) and graduated with many honours. He began his career in Edinburgh, where he established a reputation as a lecturer and skilled surgeon, his staff calling him 'The Chief', which is how he was always subsequently addressed. In 1856 Lister married Agnes Syme, the daughter of a colleague. What she thought about the honeymoon is not recorded, but the trip was apparently spent on a tour of Continental hospitals! Agnes played an important role as Lister's assistant throughout their marriage; the notebooks of his experiments are largely written by her.

Lister moved to Glasgow in 1860 and as Surgeon to the Royal Infirmary began to put into practice his belief that germs caused infections, choosing carbolic acid as his germicide. The post-operative death rate before this was

Sir Joseph (Lord) Lister, pioneer of antiseptic surgery.

extremely high: "through the wards...there ever stalked the spectre of Sepsis to the accompaniment of the beating of the wings of the Angel of Death". Lister's 'Antiseptic System' resulted in great improvements in the recovery rate, but despite this his work was frequently criticised. He returned to Edinburgh in 1869, where he remained until he finally moved to London in 1877, to take up the post of Professor of Clinical Surgery at King's College. He still had to overcome considerable opposition among London medical men and it was many years before his antiseptic procedures were fully accepted. He retired from the College in 1892. The following year, when on holiday in Italy, his wife contracted pneumonia and died 4 days later, leaving Joseph overwhelmed by grief. They lived at 12 Park Crescent, Regent's Park.

Lister received many honours from all over the world and was raised to the peerage in 1897 as Baron Lister of Lyme Regis (he owned a house there, and was very fond of the town). He maintained an active interest in medicine until 1903, when his health declined and he retired to spend most of his time at Walmer in Kent. Though offered burial in Westminster Abbey, Lister opted for this modest West Hampstead grave, where his wife already lay. He died aged 84 at Walmer, and an impressive service for him was held in Westminster Abbey. There is a good bust of him in Portland Place, near his old home, done by Sir Thomas Brock.

35c Sir Ralph Littler

(d. 23.11.1908)

WC428

Barrister, and Chairman
of the Middlesex County Council

Littler was educated at University College School and UCL. He became a barrister and worked in Northumberland before returning to the Bar in London. He was often criticised by the press, as he tended to give long sentences to the habitual criminal, even for small offences. At the time of his death he was taking proceedings for libel against two newspapers. Littler was a high-ranking freemason, Chairman of Middlesex County Council from 1889, and knighted in 1902. He died at his home, 89 Oakwood Court, Kensington.

36c James Logan Lobley

(d. 27.6.1913)

H10/94

Geologist

Professor Lobley contributed a chapter on the geology of Hampstead to Thomas Barratt's famous three-volume work *The Annals of Hampstead* (1912). He lived in Fordwych Road and Palace Street, Buckingham Gate.

37e Niels M Lund

(d. 28.2.1916)

M11/97

Artist

Born in 1863, Niels was educated at the Royal Academy Schools in London, and in Paris. Lund first exhibited at the Royal Academy in 1887 and his pictures are in galleries in Paris and Luxembourg. Note the artist's palette on the gravestone. He lived at 169 Adelaide Road.

38a Joseph Maas

(1847–1886)

D11/94–95. *EH Listed.*

Opera singer

His epitaph reads "Erected by friends and admirers in memory of a great singer and a good man". Born at Dartford and descended from an old Dutch family, Joseph studied music in Italy, making his debut in London in 1871. His fine tenor voice guaranteed him success despite his apparently indifferent acting abilities. He created the role of the Chevalier des Grieux in Massenet's *Manon* in 1885, and was much praised for his singing of Handel's Oratorios and English Ballads. Joseph died in London of rheumatic fever. A Maas memorial prize was established at the Royal Academy of Music, and there is a memorial in Rochester Cathedral where he was a chorister and soloist as a young boy.

His imposing memorial erected 6 months after his death features a life-size female figure of Music, leaning on three volumes of *Arie*, *Oratorii* and *Opere*. These rest on a pedestal which carries a relief portrait of the tenor surmounted by a laurel wreath. Maas lived at 21 Marlborough Hill.

39a Sir George Alexander MacFarren
(d. 31.10.1887)
WB445
Composer and teacher
Born in London, the son of a dancing master, MacFarren studied at the Royal Academy of Music where he later became a professor and in 1875 was elected its principal. He enjoyed a long and successful career which was marred but not interrupted by blindness. He founded The Handel Society (1844). In addition to many classical pieces, he composed music for a number of farces and melodramas. *Devil's Opera (*1838) was one of his best dramatic works; his father did the libretto, a collaboration repeated for several other works. The cantata *May Day* (1857) and the opera *Robin Hood* (1860) are also considered to be among his finest pieces. However, MacFarren exercised little influence as a composer either during or after his lifetime.

*Sir **George Alexander MacFarren**, composer and teacher.*

MacFarren's memorial service took place at Westminster Abbey, but he was refused burial there. His wife Clarina – a noted contralto singer and translator – having first disputed the charge for her husband's headstone, next wanted to plant an Austrian pine tree behind and between her husband's grave at Hampstead and that of Walter Bache (see **D.4**) in the next row. The Burial Board refused permission, despite a letter of support from Miss Bache. The MacFarrens lived at 7 Hamilton Terrace.

40a Henry MacNaughton-Jones
(d. 16.4.1918)
WA373
Doctor and poet
The interesting poem on the headstone was written by the grave's occupant. A medical man, born and raised in Cork, he founded the city's Eye, Ear and Throat Hospital in 1868 and the Cork Maternity Hospital in 1872. He moved to London in 1883, where he continued a successful career. His *Who's Who* entry lists writing verse as a hobby, and this poem entitled *The Race of Life* was one of ten that appeared in a slim volume published in 1908. He seems to have lived in Sandwell Mansions, West Hampstead, at one time but he died in Barnet aged 73.

A Florence Mary MacNaughton-Jones (d. 1889) is buried in another grave (C8/131) and she has the unusual epitaph "In Her Seventh Heaven".

41c Caroline Maud Marsh
(d. 12.2.1899)
WC420
Actress
Born in London as Caroline Maude Foster, she made her name on the American stage. Her husband Richard Marsh was the son of a noted English Shakespearean actor, Henry Marston (real name Richard Henry Marsh). After starting a career as a performer, Richard moved to America where he became a well-known set designer and presumably met his wife. Caroline died in New York and it is possible that Richard was intending to return home to England, hence her burial in London. He was living in Tufnell Park at the time but later went back to the USA, where he died in 1917. The epitaph is by American poet Fitz-Greene Halleck, taken from his *Ode on the Death of Joseph Rodman Drake.*

42e Flora Macdonald Mayor
(1872–1932)
K11/55
(Difficult to find. First turn left down the side path and locate Jennings, the first grave in front row, very overgrown, next to Kelly. Mayor is behind and to the left, completely hidden by the bushes.)
Author
Flora was one of the twin daughters of Rev. Joseph Mayor, Professor at King's College, London, and Jessie Grote, a gifted linguist. She often visited Hampstead as a child, staying with her seven unmarried aunts in Gayton Crescent. Flora received a degree from Newnham College but she suffered from chronic asthma, which made it hard for her to take up regular employment. She tried an acting career, seemingly in an attempt to break away from what she saw as an unfulfilling, middle-class lifestyle, but met with little success. It ended when she became engaged to Ernest Shepherd, a childhood friend of her brother's, who sadly died only 6 months later while on a visit to India. She

found success as a novelist (sometimes writing under the name of Mary Stafford), and her two best-known novels were *The Third Miss Symons* and *The Rector's Daughter*.

Flora lived for most of her life with her family, finally settling in 1927 with her sister Alice, at 7 East Heath Road. She died there in 1932, having contracted pneumonia and 'flu on top of her asthma. Her headstone bears the faint words from Bach's B Minor Mass "Exspecto Resurrectionem". All but one of her aunts are buried in the next row.

43c Justin McCarthy

(1830–1912)
WC433

Irish patriot, writer, novelist, historian and MP

Born near Cork, family poverty frustrated his wish to read for the Bar and at 17 he began work as a journalist with the *Cork Examiner*. He moved to England and joined the *Northern Daily Times* in Liverpool in 1854. In 1859 he moved to London, working with the *Morning Star* and became its editor in 1864. He published a number of successful novels and he was so well received on a visit to the USA that he considered living there. However, his interest in politics drew him back to London in 1871 to serve in the Irish Party under Parnell. He continued making his living as a novelist and leader writer for the Daily News. His *History of Our Own Times* (1879) established him as a popular historian and he also wrote biographies of Gladstone and Sir Robert Peel.

Justin McCarthy, Irish patriot writer, novelist, historian and MP.

In 1879 he was elected MP for Longford County. He was also MP for Derry City (1886–92) and North Longford (1892–1900) and he served as Chairman of the Irish Parliamentary Party (1890–1896). He was selected more for his balanced views rather than any great gifts as an orator. When the party split over Parnell's involvement in the O'Shea divorce case, McCarthy led the anti-Parnell group, though he managed to avoid personal recriminations and remained on friendly terms with Parnell. However, the strain of work made him ill and he became almost totally blind in 1897. He left political life in 1900 and was awarded a Civil List pension of £300 a year by the Prime Minister, Balfour. McCarthy continued to dictate his novels until 1911, though with less success than before.

He died in Folkestone, and one obituary noted it was "hard to say if he [was] to be regarded mainly as a literary man or as a politician". The view of a meeting of Irish Nationalists was that he should be buried in Ireland, but his family had already arranged burial at Hampstead Cemetery alongside his wife, who died in 1879 while the couple were living in Gower Street. The Irish Party MPs escorted the coffin from Charing Cross to Fortune Green and sent a floral tribute in the shape of a harp. McCarthy died without having made a will, and despite his success as a novelist, left an estate valued at just £460.

Justin Huntly McCarthy (d.1936)

The son of Justin McCarthy is also buried here. Justin Huntly was educated at UCS and UCL. Like his father he became a journalist and a playwright. *If I were King* and *The Candidate* were his best-known works for the stage. He travelled widely in Europe, America and the Middle East. Following in his father's footsteps he was elected a Nationalist MP (1884–1894), but he considered writing to be the most important part of his life. He died at his home in Putney, but was buried here with his father.

44c Joan Moggridge

(d. 1904)
G1/108
EH Listed.

An attractive terracotta Celtic cross with a moulded vine-and-grapes design, the symbol of Christ and his followers. Nothing is known about Joan, apart from the fact that she lived in Belsize Square.

Section D

45e Rt. Hon. Arnold Morley

(d. 1916)

K2/68

MP, Privy Councillor and Postmaster General

Arnold was the son of Samuel Morley, who had a hosiery business in London and Nottingham, and several mills in Leicestershire, Nottinghamshire and Derbyshire, employing thousands of workers. His house in Stamford Hill became the focus for dissenting religious ministers and radical politicians. Samuel was involved in the temperance movement and spent large amounts of money building chapels. In Parliament he represented Bristol and was a strong supporter of Gladstone. A rich man, Samuel bequeathed a large fortune to his eight children.

Arnold Morley was his fourth son. Educated at Trinity College, Cambridge, he became a barrister in 1873. Then, like his father, Arnold entered politics and was MP for Nottingham 1880–5 and Nottingham East 1885–95. Under Gladstone he became the chief Liberal Whip 1886–1892, and was appointed Postmaster General 1892–1895. He lived in Stratton Street, Piccadilly.

46a David Christie Murray

(1847–1907)

D12/62 (No visible grave)

Novelist and journalist

Murray was born and grew up in the Midlands. He began work in his father's printing office aged 12 and then started his career in journalism. He joined the staff of the *Birmingham Morning News*, reporting court cases at 25 shillings a week. In 1865 he enlisted in the Irish Dragoon Guards and went to Ireland, but after a year a great-aunt purchased his discharge. He then worked for various London newspapers and travelled widely. He was a correspondent for *The Times* in the Russo-Turkish War of 1877–8 and for most of the 1880s he lived in Europe. Murray also had some success as a popular lecturer and toured Australia, New Zealand and America. From 1898 he devoted considerable energy to writing and lecturing in support of Emile Zola's defence of Dreyfus, the French officer who was wrongfully condemned for spying. He wrote a large number of very popular novels, drawing on his travels and his experience as a journalist. From his first in 1879 until his death in 1907 he published one or two novels a year.

47a Joseph Haydn Parry

(1864–1894)

E9/110

Welsh composer

Son of Joseph Parry, Joseph Haydn followed in his father's musical footsteps. He was born in Pennsylvania, but the family returned to England about 1868. Largely taught by his father, Joseph Haydn became a professor at the Guildhall School of Music. He wrote three operas, all with intriguing titles – *Cigarette* (1892), *Miami* (1893) and *Marigold's Farm*. *Cigarette* is set in France about 1805 and is described as a light romantic opera. The plot is a variant of the Romeo and Juliet theme, but this time the lovers do not die but reconcile their feuding families and get married. *Cigarette* is the heroine, while Nicotine also appears as the village braggart!

The tombstone says *His sun set while it was still day*, a reference to his youth: Parry was only 30 when he died at his home, 87 Broadhurst Gardens. His epitaph is from the hymn *Abide With Me*. Parry had been working on a new musical setting of the hymn just before he died. Also note the lyre engraved on the headstone.

48e Perigrine Platt

(d. 1909)

M1/93

Manager of Field Lane School, Hillfield Road

The Field Lane Institution was started in 1841, to teach poor children from the Holborn slums. Thirty years later two residential Industrial Schools were set up, taking in destitute or abandoned children, orphans and young offenders. Educated and trained in various skills such as tailoring, shoemaking, carpentry and baking, jobs were found for them when they left the school aged 16. In 1878 the schools moved to Hampstead – the girls to Church Row and the boys to a new building in Hillfield Road opposite the junction with Aldred Road (closed 1931). Locals still remember seeing the boys marching round the streets in an orderly crocodile, and threatened to send their own children to the school if they were naughty. Platt was Secretary of The Field Lane Institution, Clerkenwell, for 35 years.

49e Thomas Potter

(d. 1917)

WC469A

(On Rishworth stone, in front row)

Iron founder

This is the grave of the Potter family, the children of Thomas Potter Sr who built an iron foundry in the village of West End about 1860, opposite West End Green and roughly on the site of the present Welbeck Mansions. The flats, which date from about 1896, are named after one of Potter's wealthiest clients, the Duke of Portland, whose home was Welbeck Abbey. The nearby West Cottages were built by Potter to house his workers. Until shortly before its demolition in 1891 the family lived in 'Poplar House', a large mansion which stood near the present junction of Inglewood Road and West End Lane, although the father had earlier retired to Sussex. Thomas Potter Jr, who is also buried here, moved to Pattison Road, but died in Peckham Lunatic Asylum.

50c Edith Poutiatine

(d. 1928)

G8/108

Russian Countess

The inscription says that two Countess Poutiatine are buried here: Elizabeth (born 1863), and Edith Poutiatine (née Cazalet, born 1866), who was the mother of Vera Poutiatine. At one time they lived at 54 The Pryors. We have not been able to resolve exactly who the Poutiatines were. It seems probable that Edith and Elizabeth were the daughters of Edward Alexander Cazalet. He worked with his father Alexander, who set up 'A. Cazalet and Sons' in St Petersburg. Edward (d.1923), was a linguist who travelled repeatedly to Russia, Persia and Turkey, and was the founder and president of the Anglo-Russian Literary Society. At the time of the births of Elizabeth and Edith, Edward Cazalet was working for the Russian Steam Navigation and Trading Company at Odessa.

It has not been possible to discover how both Edith and Elizabeth became Countess Poutiatine, nor is there much information about the Poutiatine family, apart from the fact that a Sergei Mikhailovitch, Prince Poutiatine, was born in St Petersburg in 1896. He was the second husband of Grand Duchess Maria Pavlovna Romanov (1890–1958) and he died in South Carolina in 1966.

51c Sir Richard Quain

(d. 13.3.1898)

WA430

Physician extraordinary to Queen Victoria

Irish-born, he entered University College London, where his cousins Jones and Richard Quain were teaching anatomy. The author of many medical works, he was chairman of the committee that produced the standard work on drugs, the *British Pharmacopoeia*, and the editor of the *Dictionary of Medicine*. He was a Consultant to the Brompton Chest Hospital and the Seamen's Hospital in Greenwich. Quain was a Fellow of the Royal Society and elected President of the General Medical Council in 1891, the same year he was created a baronet. Quain had a fashionable practice which included Thomas Carlyle and Sir Edwin Landseer. His portrait by Millais is in the Royal College of Physicians. He lived at 67 Harley Street.

Justin McCarthy (see **D.43**) recalled a dinner date with Quain: "Nobody could tell a good story better, no one could freshen up a good story into such new and animated life...there was the sunny freshness of what seemed an everlasting youth about him....He was a welcome guest at all the houses of all the highest personages in the land...and I know that he brought good cheer into the homes of his poorest patients".

52c Dolph Rieser

(1898–1983)

G10/122

Artist, etcher and engraver

Born in South Africa, Rieser studied in Munich and Lausanne, gaining a doctorate in plant genetics. But he became a painter in the 1920s and in Paris he studied engraving under Joseph Hecht. His work was influenced by the cave paintings of African bushmen which he fused with surrealism. A strong critic of Fascism, Rieser fled Paris the day the Nazis entered the city. He came to London and offered his knowledge of French and German to help Special Operations intelligence. After the war he developed two new techniques of colour printing and printing onto plastic. This combination of art and science dominated his work for the next 30 years. Rieser had over 20 one-man shows and his 400 works are exhibited in many of the world's art galleries. He lived in Sumatra Road, West Hampstead.

53c Henry Parsons Riviere
(1811–1888)
G8/131
(Grave is inaccessible, covered by dense undergrowth)
Artist

Born in Marylebone, the son of a drawing master, Riviere became a student at the Royal Academy and he also painted at the Artists' Society in Clipstone Street. In 1834 he was elected a member of the New Society of Painters in Watercolour, where he exhibited over 100 drawings during the next 16 years. Many of his subjects were of Irish life and humour with titles such as *A Bit of Blarney*. About 1865 he gave up work as a teacher and went to Rome, where he drew the ancient ruins. He was an able copyist of Old Masters and produced hundreds of drawings which were exhibited at the Royal Academy, the British Institution and the Society of British Artists. In 1884 he finally returned to England and he died at his home, 26 St John's Wood Road, in May 1888.

54a William Roper
(d. 14.5.1891)
C12/79–80
Owner of Bon Marché shop in Kilburn

William founded the Kilburn Bon Marché, a well-known drapery and furnishing business which traded from a number of shops on Kilburn High Road, south of Belsize Road. With the help of his wife Stephanie (who was always addressed as Madame Roper) he was a founder member of St James's Church, West End Lane. As his grave is adjacent to that of Mr Saner (see **D.57**) who played a similar role, it seems likely the two families were friends. The Ropers lived in 'Cricklewood House', a mansion set in extensive grounds at the junction of Edgware Road and Cricklewood Lane. On the occasion of their Silver Wedding in 1889, a huge marquee was put up in their back garden "providing bathroom, dining room, and side rooms". The celebrations stretched over 3 days, the Ropers inviting their shop staff as well as friends and family. "The fine figure of the owner of The Kilburn Bon Marché was a familiar sight along the Edgware Road, as he took part of his favourite horse exercise in journeying between his house of business and his residence". Roper died in May 1891 after a long illness following an accident. Most of the Kilburn businesses shut down for his funeral. Mme Roper donated the font to St James's and later a window in William's memory, representing the nine orders of angels. She moved to Elsworthy Road, where she rather confusingly christened her new home 'Cricklewood House'.

55a Alexander Ross
(d. 3.2.1923)
C12/87
President of Institution of Civil Engineers

Elected President of the Institution of Civil Engineers 1915–1916, Ross had pursued a successful career as a civil engineer, working for several railway companies in the UK until 1911, when he set up as an independent consultant. He lived at 36 Fellows Road.

56a Anthony Roth
(1943–1992)
WB427
Art dealer and historian

Born in Los Angeles, the son of a wealthy émigré diamond merchant, Roth studied art at Harvard and Princeton. A talented scholar, he helped catalogue the flood damage in Florence in 1966 and went on to become an authority on medals. He was described as "witty and black-humoured (with) an extraordinary knowledge of art".

In 1984 he opened a London gallery in Maddox Street, later moving to larger premises in South Street, Mayfair. But it was his knack of making sensational art discoveries that put him in the public eye. Perhaps the best known is the terracotta figure by Andrea del Verrocchio, the sculptor and painter to whom Leonardo da Vinci was apprenticed. Roth found the sculpture in a cardboard box with a kettle and other items in the Portobello Road and bought it for £50. This turned out to be the original model for *The Executioner of St John the Baptist* worth millions, but it took Roth 3 years to prove the figure was genuine and dated to 1478. In 1999 the male torso left the country, as none of the British galleries or museums could raise the £2 million required to purchase it. Roth also discovered an early work by Bernini and one of his contemporaries Francesco Mochi. Roth lived locally at 49 Parkhill Road.

57a John Saner
(d. 24.11.1889)
C11/83–85
A founder of St James', Sherriff Road
Sometimes referred to as Lieutenant Colonel, reflecting his voluntary service rank in the Yorkshire Yeomanry, John Saner was a wealthy landowner who lived in Hull for most of his life. A JP and Director of the Hull Dock Company, Saner moved to London only a few years before his death. He bought 'Whitefriars', a large house in what was then called Chislett Road (now 77 Compayne Gardens) and, with others, promoted the building of St James', West End Lane. The site was just a short walk from his home. He later took over as the Hon. Secretary of the building fund and became its first warden. All the nearby shops closed as a mark of respect during his funeral service and there is a window in the church dedicated to his memory.

58c Ernest Joseph Schuster
(d. 1924)
WB497
Barrister
Born in Frankfurt, the son of a banker, Ernest was educated in Germany and Switzerland. He was a barrister with his firm of Schuster, Son and Co. in Cannon Street. He also served on various professional bodies, wrote widely on legal matters and necame a barrister in 1922. Ernest was Stephen Spender's maternal grandfather. Spender remembered how as a young boy he and his family would regularly walk on Sundays the four or five miles from his home in Frognal to Schuster's home in Albert Court, behind the Albert Hall (see also Spender, **D.62**).

59a William Booth Scott
(d. 1891)
E11/109–110
Surveyor
Scott was Chief Surveyor of St Pancras during a time of transformation, when its open fields were being covered by streets and houses. He both witnessed and guided many of these changes. In 1890 his *St Pancras Local Management* was published, a book which Scott himself admitted was "egotistic in tenor". However, it contains much valuable information on the history of St Pancras: its main roads, their improvement and management; private roads and paving boards; tramways, disused burial grounds and open spaces; bridges, railways and much more. Scott lived at 16 Church Row and died suddenly just a few months after his wife.

60c Edward Searle
(d. 1887)
G8/129
(Grave is inaccessible, covered by dense undergrowth)
Boat builder
Edward Searle was one of a family of boat builders based at Stangate, Lambeth (the site of St Thomas's Hospital). The firm moved to Henley-on-Thames shortly after Edward died, meriting a mention in Dickens' *Sketches by Boz*: "What can be more amusing than Searle's yard on a fine Sunday morning? It's a Richmond tide, and some dozen boats are preparing for the reception of parties who have engaged them." It is likely they had other boat-houses on the river, at Eton and Putney.

George Searle had established his Lambeth business by 1777, trading under the name Searle and Sons. It seems probable that Edward was his grandson. The firm was appointed Boat Builder to most of the crowned heads of Europe, including Queen Victoria, and Edward succeeded his father as bargemaster to several Lord Mayors of London. They manufactured all types of pleasure craft and rowing boats, including those used in several University Boat Races. Edward actually started the race on many occasions and in 1841 he also built both boats! Although he was not the main inventor, Searle held a patent for a sliding seat, using the principle of a piece of wood sliding in channels fixed to the seat to give the rower extra leverage; Searle's version used glass runners. Slides were not widely used in England until the 1870s, but reports indicate that Searle eventually succeeded in incorporating them and improved the performance of his boats. His obituary noted that he also enjoyed "the privilege of having his pleasure crafts in the ornamental water at Regent's Park [just across the road from his house] and various other places". Searle was 78 when he died at his home in Park Road.

Section D

61a Henry Thomas Smart
(d. 6.7.1879)
E9/111

Composer and organist

Henry Thomas was one of a talented family of musicians. His father Henry (d.1823) was a violinist and music publisher who had a piano factory in Berners Street. His uncle Charles played the double bass and a second uncle, Sir George Smart (d.1867), was a conductor. Young Smart was sent to boarding school at Lauderdale House, Highgate. After abandoning the army and the law in favour of a musical career, he underwent some formal training, but was largely self-taught. Smart was an excellent organ player and while his best works were composed for that instrument, he also did choral works and operas. In 1865 he became organist at St Pancras Church, where he had been married in 1840. At that time the musical part of the service was very simple and Smart's accompaniments and extemporisation attracted many musicians to the Church. He held the post until his death in 1879 after a long illness. Smart had been blind for several years and died before he could enjoy a Government pension awarded in acknowledgement of his services to music. He lived at 30 King Henry's Road.

Henry Thomas Smart, composer and organist.

62c Edward Harold Spender
(d. 15.4.1926)
WB499

Author and journalist, father of Sir Stephen Spender the poet

Educated at Oxford, Edward became a professional journalist, writing books and articles on politics and travel as well as three biographies on Asquith, General Louis Botha and Lloyd George. He also contested Bath as a Liberal MP in 1922. The family lived at 10 Frognal where his son Stephen attended nearby University College School. Violet Schuster, Stephen's mother, died when the boy was only 12 and his father Edward died 5 years later. Like his father, Stephen went to Oxford and pursued a literary career. He served as a fireman during WW II, and for a while was based in Maresfield Gardens in the company of the writer William Sansom. Stephen published a large number of books and essays and was awarded the Queen's Gold Medal for Poetry in 1971. Knighted in 1983, he lived at 15 Loudoun Road until his death in 1995. (See also Schuster, **D.58**).

63c Margaret Stapfer
(d. 1886)
J2/106

A very interesting pyramid-shaped memorial with no apparent inscription. Margaret, the wife of Professor Stapfer, lived in Marlborough Road.

64c Henry Stevens
(d. 1886)
F11/121

Dealer in rare books

Born in Barnet in Vermont USA. The substantial monument marking Stevens' grave was made in Montpelier, about 30 miles from his birthplace. Stevens worked as a clerk in the Senate House, Washington DC, later supporting himself through 3 years of college by teaching writing in his spare time. He graduated from Yale, then studied law at Harvard and came to London in 1845, "with a few Yankee notions in his head and nearly 40 gold sovereigns in his pocket". Stevens' interest was in American rare books and pamphlets and he soon become the main supplier of these to the British Museum, producing a catalogue of the same, and later diversifying to include English material. Stevens also wrote extensively on rare books and bibliographic matters. He died at his home, the appropriately named 'Vermont', 13 Avenue Road.

65a Lt-Col John Wilfred Stokes
(d. 10.2.1916)
C8/139
Soldier, died of shell shock
Probably the only epitaph in Hampstead Cemetery to actually refer to 'shell shock' as a cause of death. Having qualified from University College Hospital, Stokes went to work as a GP in Sheffield, where he was also a demonstrator in anatomy at the University and the Royal Infirmary. During the war he was attached to the Royal Army Medical Corps (TF) 3rd West Riding Field Ambulance, and he died in France. An obituary praised his "geniality and quiet humour, coupled with a frank, straightforward disposition". The grave was bought by Rev. Arthur Stokes, who lived at 10 Canfield Gardens.

66c John Matthias Augustus Stroh
(d. 3.11.1914)
WB453
Inventor of an acoustic violin
John Stroh turned out to be a natural-born inventor in almost every scientific field, including electricity and magnetism, optics and horology. Born in Frankfurt, he worked as an apprentice watchmaker before emigrating to England in the 1850s. He worked closely with Charles (later Sir Charles) Wheatstone, contributing to his many improvements in telegraphy. In 1860 Stroh set up a factory at Tolmers Square (just off Euston Road) to manufacture his and Wheatstone's instruments. He retired 20 years later but opened a workshop in his Haverstock Hill home and went on inventing.

His violin patented in 1901 was designed to solve a specific problem. At this time there was no amplification of sound prior to its recording. The performer played into a horn, the sound waves vibrating a diaphragm at the end of the horn where an attached stylus cut a groove into soft wax. Violins were often drowned out by other sounds, and a louder instrument was needed. Stroh replaced the violin's sound-box with an aluminium diaphragm and large trumpet horn. This could be moved and directed towards the recording horn. It was very successful, though not without its critics. Fred Gaisberg (see **C.9**), who was involved in early recordings, claimed that a Stroh violin soloist had to "exaggerate heavily the pizzicato, glissando and vibrato characteristics of his instrument" in order to be heard. Improvements to recording techniques rendered the Stroh violin redundant so far as the studio was concerned, but they went on being made (in Albany Street) and used for live performances until the 1940s. Stroh left an estate worth £93,901.

67a Rev. Francis William Tremlett
(d. 1913)
F1/94
Vicar of St Peter's, Belsize Square
Tremlett was one of Hampstead's longest-serving vicars. He donated the cost of building the nave, aisles and transept of St Peter's and remained as vicar for over half a century, from 1860 until his death in 1913. Aside from this longevity he can make a good claim to be the district's most unusual cleric. Many of those attending his funeral service were probably unaware that Tremlett had been an ardent supporter of the Southern cause in the American Civil War. In the 1860s he was Secretary to the "Society for Obtaining the Cessation of Hostilities in America" and his home became a refuge for Confederate spies and other military personnel. He even found local accommodation for the crew of the *Alabama*, a Confederate ship sunk off Cherbourg in 1864.

68c Florence Upton

(d. 1922)

J12/58

(Locate James Walsh's grave on front row; behind is a path, and Upton is three graves back, to the left. Stone is currently laid flat.)

Painter and creator of the Golliwogg [sic]

The inscription reads "Of New York and Westminster... She was possessed of a gift of fantasy and created the Golliwogg to the unfading delight of generations of children". (Note the original spelling which uses two 'g's and a capital letter.) Florence's parents, Thomas Harborough Upton and Bertha Hudson, were both English but were married in New York where Thomas was working. Florence was one of four children and the family remained in America after Thomas's death in 1889. In 1893 they made a visit to England to stay with Bertha's parents in her old home in Fellows Road, and it was here that Florence invented the 'Golliwogg'. Aware of her mother's financial problems, she decided to write a children's story. She found some wooden Dutch dolls and they became Sarah Jane, Peg, Meg, Weg and Midget but the tale needed a 'hero'. Then she unearthed an old Afro-American doll in the attic which she transformed into the 'Golliwogg.' Florence drew the pictures and her mother Bertha wrote the text. It took some time to find a publisher, but the stories proved a great success with children. They included *The Golliwogg's Auto-Go-Cart* and *The Golliwogg's Fox Hunt* with an interesting alternative entitled *The Vege-Men's Revenge*. The last book was published in 1909.

Florence did not patent the Golliwogg and although she made a lot of money from her books, others were quick to cash in on their popularity. The figure of the Golliwogg appeared on a range of products such as wallpaper, Christmas cards and paperweights and in recent memory, pots of Robertson's jam. In 1906-8 Debussy composed *Children's Corner* for his daughter and called the last movement *Golliwogg's cake walk*. The original dolls were sold at a Christie's auction in 1917 in aid of the Red Cross and together with 350 of Florence's drawings, they raised enough money to buy and equip an ambulance which went to the Front in France. On it was painted the inscription "Florence Upton and the Golliwoggs gave this ambulance".

Her artistic achievements are sometimes overlooked, but the obituary in *The Times* described her as "first a painter and second a children's book illustrator". After the Golliwogg books were launched, Florence continued her studies in Paris and then in Holland under George Hitchcock. She exhibited at the Salon and Royal Academy and is best known for her portraits. In later life she also took a great interest in spiritualism and spirit writing. Florence lived and worked in Westminster, at 21 Great College Street.

***Florence Upton**, creator of the 'Golliwogg'.*

69e Rev. Marmaduke Washington

(d. 28.10.1935)

K2/67

Canon of Norwich Cathedral

Born in Derbyshire, and educated at Repton and Trinity College, Cambridge, Rev. Washington held many clerical posts up and down the country. At the time of his death he lived in Eastbourne.

70a James John Garth Wilkinson

(d. 1899)

E7/123–124

Religious writer

A member of the Royal College of Surgeons, he opened a homeopathic clinic in Wimpole Street. But he was attracted by the writings of William Blake and in 1839 edited the *Songs of Innocence and Experience* with considerable alterations. He became a member of the Committee of the Swedenborg Society and devoted himself to the translation and publication of Swedenborg's writings. His work was greatly admired by Ralph Waldo Emerson and he became a friend of Carlyle, Dickens, and Tennyson. Wilkinson travelled widely in Europe, Scandinavia and America. His first London house was at 25 Church Row and he died at his home, 4 Finchley Road.

71c Sir Samuel Wilks

(d. 8.11.1911)

G4/114

Physician extraordinary to Queen Victoria

Wilks was born in South London and studied at Guy's Hospital, where he became a physician and curator of the museum. He published numerous papers and was an early researcher on Hodgkin's disease. Much of his work was on the history of medicine. From 1896 to 1899 he was elected President of the Royal College of Physicians and a portrait of him by Percy Ryland hangs in the College dining room. In 1897 Wilks was created a baronet and appointed physician extraordinary to Queen Victoria. From 1901 until his death he lived at 8 Prince Arthur Road.

72c Rear Adm. Charles Woodwright

(d. 2.5.1949)

G9/111

Surgeon Rear Admiral RN

Born in 1870 the son of a colonel of the 18th Royal Irish Regiment, Charles served in the blockade of Crete in 1896. During WW I he was mentioned in dispatches and awarded the CBE in 1919.

73c Frederick Wright

(d. 19.10.1911)

H8/119

Actor and manager

When Frederick Wright died aged 85, he was thought to be the oldest actor still working. He first appeared in 1854 and at the age of 76 he even went on a US tour. For many years he was the manager of an Edinburgh theatre but he also ran his own touring companies, a fact acknowledged by his obituary which called him "the father of the touring companies". Frederick personally trained his five children for their vocation as actors. At his funeral wreaths were sent by Sir Herbert Beerbohm Tree and Mr and Mrs Fred Terry. He lived at 42 Stanley Gardens, Belsize Park, and left a will totalling only £400.

His daughter Haidee made her first stage appearance as a child and had a success as the boy martyr in *The Sign of The Cross* (1896), a play written by Wilson Barrett (see Section B). She died, aged 75, in 1943 and is buried here with her parents. Frederick Wright Jr, who is not buried here, also became an actor and vocalist. He died in 1919 and his will of £15,700 suggests he was more financially successful than his father. Another son, Huntley Wright, was a very popular comedian, singer and dancer and a regular performer at Daly's Theatre in Leicester Square. He appeared in *A Country Girl* in 1902, which ran for over 700 performances. He died in 1943 and left a will of £19,500.

74a Sarah Edith Wynne

(1842–1897)

E5/131

Welsh soprano singer

Buried here under her married name of Agabeg, Sarah Wynne studied in Italy and at the Royal College of Music. Known as the 'Welsh Nightingale', she specialised in songs and ballads from her homeland. She also had a noted success as the heroine *Jessie Lea*, in one of Sir George MacFarren's works (see **D.39**). Sarah married Aviet Agabeg QC and they lived for a while at 61 Boundary Road.

***Sarah Edith Wynne**, Welsh soprano.*

The Good Grave Guide
to Hampstead Cemetery, Fortune Green

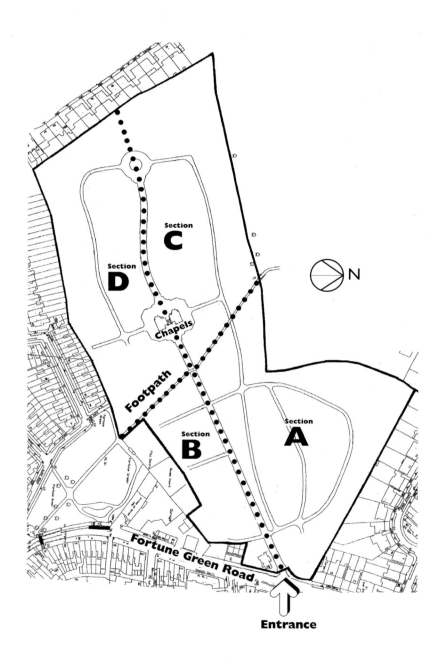

Opposite: aerial photograph showing location of the graves in Section B →
On back cover: aerial photograph showing location of the graves in Sections C & D
Underlying photograph © by Aerofilms Ltd